# Two steps back A LIFETIME forward

## A Success Guide For Modern Living

# BRYAN FIESE

simple PUBLISHING

# Two Steps Back, A Lifetime Forward
## A Success Guide for Modern Living

by Bryan R. Fiese

Published by:

**Simple Publishing** - **A Consignment Trust Company**
P.O Box 701774
Dallas, TX 75370

Editing: ABC Editing San Diego, CA
Typesetting: Barbara Allen
Cover Design: Bryan R. Fiese

Printed in United States of America

January 2000

Library of Congress Number: 99-094981

ISBN: 0-9676942-0-5

*Dedicated to all those who
supported and believed in me.*

# TABLE OF CONTENTS

" The credit belongs to the man who is actually in the arena, whose face is marred by dust, sweat and blood: who strives valiantly; who errs and comes short again, who knows the great enthusiasms, the great devotion, and spends himself in a worthy cause; who at best, knows the triumph of high achievement; and who, at worst, if he fails, at least fails while daring greatly, so that his place shall never be with those cold and timid souls who knows neither victory nor defeat. "      Theodore Roosevelt

# Introduction

For as long as I can remember I have tirelessly searched for a better way to journey through life. I never accepted things as they were. I always questioned why and how things were done. One of my most significant discoveries was learning that there truly is no right or wrong way to live. There aren't any secret formulas that ensure success. The quality of life can only be defined by individual perceptions because *your* perception is *your* reality. Many of us wander through life aimlessly, searching for inner peace and contentment, with no idea where to find it. Until one day a life-changing experience catapults us into a new realm of existence. I, myself, have had this kind of profound enlightenment.

One day, shortly after shutting down an unsuccessful business, I was eating lunch at the kitchen table, brooding over my failure, feeling somewhat vulnerable. At this particular period of my life I wasn't the most upbeat person, nor did I feel receptive to new ideas.  Quite unexpectedly and without warning, the difficult answers I had been seeking blossomed in my thoughts with crystal clarity.  The final piece to the puzzle was at my fingertips.

I was watching a news channel, listening to a story about a lunatic who had murdered his fourteen year old daughter, then killed himself with the same gun.  This tragic event both mortified and  mesmerized me.  I asked myself, "How could this happen?  What could be so bad in someone's life?"  I changed the channel.  Another news station was reporting live at the scene where two people were hit by a car and killed while fixing a flat tire at the side of a road.  As I continued to flip through the channels, looking for an uplifting story, I discovered that every news channel was reporting similar atrocities: hate crimes, murders, rapes, arson, fraud, vandalism. Controversy and sensationalism seemed to rule the news stations. I concluded that this is what people wanted to watch.   Stories like these drove the ratings. Hoping to escape from all the hate and carnage, I turned off the television and flipped on the radio, prepared to listen to some soothing music.  Quite to my dismay, I discovered that disc jockeys employed the same rating strategies as the television news channels.  Between songs they would discuss emotionally charged topics, knowing that listeners would respond and either debate or concur with the DJ's statements.  All this controversy was for one purpose: to increase ratings.

I turned off the radio and a vision crept into my thoughts.    I remembered an incident that happened not too long ago.  One day, while driving my car, observing the speed limit and minding my own business in the right lane, a car came barreling up behind me, trying to pass.  There was a car in the left lane preventing this maniac from going around me.  In my rear view mirror I could see him boiling with anger.  When he finally was able to pass me, he made an obscene gesture with his middle finger.  Why, I thought?  How could anyone be so much in a hurry that they would abandon common courtesy?  I had, at that time, the same sickening feeling I'd had when I 'd heard about the young girl killed by her father.  For years these emotions had been building up inside me; an awareness of just how hostile a world we lived in.   Finally, I understood the connection between all these incidents.  Losing my business, hearing all of the horrible news stories, and the daily task of fighting traffic, somehow helped me to uncover one of the most significant inequities in life. Our daily lives are more effected by negative external stimuli than positive. The media feeds and perpetuates this condition by focusing their coverage on unpleasant news events. These negative incidents break us down mentally and prohibit us from improving our outlook on life. Some people can manage this negative assault better than others, but in some way it effects all of us and impairs our ability to enjoy life.

At that moment I made a commitment to myself that I would no longer allow anyone else to influence my emotions with negative thoughts. I wasn't going to let sensational news reports, or radio disc jockeys, or rude drivers impact my perception of life. My new philosophy was to live for the moment; not in a reckless manner, more from a perspective to "seize the moment." I began to carefully analyze my life, painstakingly examining everything I did. During this period of self-evaluation I spent a great deal of time alone, getting inside myself, looking beyond the reflection in the mirror, closely examining the substance of who I was. I read a mountain of books; anything and everything that had a positive message. I discovered that many of the ideas I uncovered were valid, but some were so scientific that they required too much conscious effort. So, I began to look inside for answers.

I explored the factors in my life that made me smile and kept that smile. I conducted surveys, studying a wide spectrum of people, asking pointed questions about what external elements contributed to their success, and which caused them to fail. I uncovered the particulars that distinguished prosperous, fulfilled people from those unhappy with their lives.

I learned that the one common denominator that connected all these productive people was that each of them possessed a clear understanding of who they were. They were also acutely aware that the potential for failure lurked in every corner. I continued to strive for more answers, finding new ways to create happiness.

This book is a collection of these thoughts, philosophies and ideas. It is written for anyone searching for a better life. Although our educational system, neighborhood churches, employers, friends and family have attempted to support us and positively influence our lives, they have been, for the most part, incapable of teaching us how to savor life and enjoy a carefree existence. The intent of this book is for me to share my spiritual awakening with you. In formulating these simple philosophies of life, in search of self-enlightenment, I found my own answers, and I would like to share them with you. I do not wish to impose on your insights, only to plant a seed of hope that will continue to grow. If you have the desire and determination to explore new ideas, your life can become a beautiful adventure where the sun always shines and the world in which you live is abundant with smiles.

Finally, I wish to express my deepest gratitude to my parents. They have, at times, wondered if I truly had the ingredients to succeed. They have been the greatest contributors to my success and have wholeheartedly supported me with all my endeavors. One way to repay them for all their support is to share my revelations with as many people as possible. I hope that you enjoy this book, and that it inspires you to become the best you can be. If you have a special success or relationship story you would like to share, I would love to hear from you.

To Happy Living — Bryan R. Fiese.

# Chapter One:
## The River of Life

For just a moment, depart from the hustle and bustle of your life, and escape from your daily routine. Think of yourself as a winding river, like the Colorado. Feel it carve its way through the Grand Canyon with tremendous force, effortlessly pushing through the land. Millions of years ago, long before man existed, mighty rivers were formed from a single raindrop. They began their evolution from the tops of mountain peaks. As raindrops accumulated at these high elevations, they began to surge down the sides of mountains, gaining momentum and force. Streams converged at the base of these mountains, multiplying the size and power. As they flowed forward, increasing in volume and authority, they continued down the side of the terrain, off the edge of great cliffs, forming beautiful waterfalls. Then, as water gathered at the base of these mountains, it continued its journey through the low points in the land and formed rivers. Even today, centuries after Mother Nature created these mighty rivers, the magical phenomenon continues. Each day, rain and condensation quietly accumulate on the tops of mountains and forge on to feed the rivers with fresh life. This mysterious and wondrous event supports life on the planet Earth and nourishes all forms of living things.

*"Everything you can imagine is real."*
**Pablo Picasso**

## The Link

Your flow through life is much like that of a river. You began as a simple organism, similar to the singular raindrop on the peak of a mountain. At the moment of conception, you were just as seemingly insignificant as that tiny raindrop. But, like the river, you continued to grow, each day you evolved to a higher level of existence, constantly adjusting to an ever-changing environment. As time moved forward, your senses developed and you became more aware of your surroundings, until one day you were born into a world unknown.

As an adult, every day presents a new challenge, a contest that must be overcome. These challenges tax the resolve of your river, cutting their way into your path. All of your life experiences, all the roadblocks that you've had to overcome throughout your life, have helped to create and strengthen your river. You have had to push your way through unyielding obstacles, through hardship and  adversity to allow your river of life to flow freely.

Your outlook on life, the images that form in your mind's eye, determines the direction, speed, and depth of your river. The clarity and color of the water are directly related to your personal perceptions. A positive outlook creates crystal blue water. If your thoughts are negative, the water will be murky, polluting your life. No matter how unclear or muddy your river, it is never too late to purify it and transform it into a beautiful body of water. The principles in this book are time-tested. They are designed to show you how to build a pure and beautiful river of life. You will create lush river banks, lined with flourishing trees, thick vegetation, and healthy wildlife. As your river flows through life, your eyes will bask in the beauty of your surroundings.

**"What the mind can imagine and believe, the human body can achieve."**

## The Lake of Dreams

All rivers flow into larger bodies of water. At the end of your river of life there is a lake. I call it the Lake of Dreams. This larger body of water is where all your efforts bear fruit, where dreams come true. It is your final destination, a paradise where anything is possible, where all of your ambitions and aspirations become real. Whether you dream of wealth, health, family, security, love, passion, or adventure, this Lake of Dreams fulfills your lifelong desires. But this final destination is not reached without the necessary dedication and commitment required to make your dreams a reality. From start to finish, you must make prudent decisions and keep paddling toward your goals. The bigger your river, the larger and more plentiful the lake. The lake is calm, not even the slightest ripple blemishes its mirror-like surface. The stronger your current, the greater your resolve and determination, the faster you can reach the Lake of Dreams. Remember, even if your life is moving downstream, heading for the Lake of Dreams, you must constantly monitor your current to make sure it is strong enough to get you there within your lifetime. You must continue to add water and increase the force. This can only happen if you constantly take on new challenges. I would like you to carefully consider what is important to you and write these down. When you reach your Lake of Dreams, what do you want to be waiting for you? What are your goals?

| List 5 Goals |
|---|
| 1. |
| 2. |
| 3. |
| 4. |
| 5. |

*"The difference between a successful person and others is not a lack of strength, not a lack of knowledge, but rather in a lack of will."*
*-Vincent Lombardi-*

## Building Your Raft

Negotiating your way down the river, toward your Lake of Dreams, can be a treacherous journey. Even if your river is flowing effortlessly, the only way to successfully complete the trip is to prepare yourself with the proper knowledge and experience. This is not a process that happens overnight; it is on ongoing adventure. Many people begin their voyage without proper planning and preparation. Life, with all of its complexities and complications, can easily sabotage even the best laid plans. Your Raft must be built with quality materials that will endure unexpected storms and all the hardships associated with life.

I often speak to high school students, and one of the most frequently asked questions is, "Is a college education important?" My answer, of course, has always been, "Yes." But I preface my answer by telling these students that a formal education is merely the beginning. Life is all about learning; a never-ending process. If you stop learning, your expedition down your river ends before you reach your Lake of Dreams.

There are those who claim to be bored with learning. This, for the most part, is because their lives lack adventure. The thrill of learning something new, particularly when it is something that excites you, fosters enthusiasm. For us to grow and develop, we must learn those things that will nourish us and improve the quality of life. If you have strong religious convictions, perhaps reading the Bible would be inspiring. Or maybe you've always wanted to play the piano, or learn to sail, or write poetry. Whatever the case, remember that today is the first day of the rest of your life, and to squander even a minute is senseless. One of the most consistent problems with conventional education is that many youngsters are forced to learn things that don't appeal to them. This often gives them a negative overall impression of education.

> **"A great pleasure in life is doing what**
> **people say you cannot do."**
> **Walter Gagehot**

In 1990, Charles Bangum graduated from high school in a small town in Southern California. School never came easy to him. He explained that math and science were such a struggle, he was amazed he had actually graduated. When asked if he was going to college, he replied, "No, I barely made it through high school. I'm just not smart like everybody else. I'm not good with science and can't even do math without pulling out my hair." Charles was absolutely right. He performed poorly in those subjects, but failed to recognize that he excelled in English, Art, and History, and was remarkably creative and imaginative. The point is that those two subjects eclipsed his perception of his academic performance to a point that made him conclude he was an inferior student.

The moral of the story is this: You should not limit your expectations and assume an incorrect identity based on those things in which you do not excel. Your thinking must be modified to focus your efforts on subjects that transcend the norm. This does not suggest that you totally abandon those subjects that were difficult. Only that you concentrate and continue to learn more about those for which you have a natural talent. Know your limitations, but continue to strengthen your weaknesses. Start to think about learning as a positive experience.

Examine the five goals you listed above. What knowledge are you lacking that might prohibit you from reaching your Lake of Dreams? What can you do to ensure that you achieve all of your goals? The more knowledge and experience you possess, the greater the chances for success. The stronger your raft, the greater the possibility you will make it to the end of the river. Analyze what is required for you to reach your final destination. Have you built a strong enough raft? What five new skills will you need to learn to ensure that your raft will help you reach the Lake of Dreams?

| Five New Skills You Will Develop |
| --- |
| 1. |
| 2. |
| 3. |
| 4. |
| 5. |

*"We cannot become what we want to be,*
*by remaining what we are."*
*-Max Dupree-*

## The Adventure

Now that you have worked hard to create your river and build your raft, imagine yourself standing at the water's edge, ready to take the plunge and begin the journey. Can you feel the exhilaration? This is a monumental turning point in your life, one that discards old ideas and embraces a new way of thinking. Once you place the raft in the water, you must make a steadfast commitment to yourself. Don't cut yourself short. The ride will have bends and curves and rapids. Be careful not to rush the ride. Enjoy the voyage. Savor the scenery. Rejoice in life.

A close friend of mine operates a recruiting business, placing medical professionals. Her career is demanding and she works from sun up to sun down, spending countless hours interviewing clients seeking employment. Most people admire her drive and dedication. The financial rewards of her successful business are substantial, and she also derives great personal satisfaction knowing that she was instrumental in helping others find work. Each day is a grind: meeting clients, setting up interviews, following up, returning numerous telephone calls. There never seems to be enough hours in her day.

I walked into her office one day, surprised to find her with her head down on her desk, crying. "I am going crazy," she said. "Every day I work and work, trying to make things happen. I don't think I can continue this way. I'm driving myself crazy!"

"You're absolutely right," I replied.

She explained how she gives everything to her applicants and clients, making sure they are happy.

"What about you?" I asked. "You're sitting here with ulcers, and your stomach is always hurting. Why not do what makes you happy?  How about enjoying the day?"

After a long silence and a deep sigh, she said, "Unfortunately, that doesn't pay the bills."

"You need to slow down," I said. "Look around. You have a nice place to live, you're healthy, you have family and friends, and whenever you choose you can walk outside and enjoy a sunset.  Think about how you'd feel if every morning you had to work for someone else.  Working under their schedule and demands.  You have your own business.  Stop hurrying through the day and start enjoying the fact that you are providing for yourself.  I'd be willing to bet that most people would trade their position with you in a heartbeat."

I could see that my words were starting to make sense.  Reflect on the positive things in your life. Be grateful for the opportunity just to be alive. It's so easy to get bogged down with the struggles of today. To enjoy life you need to appreciate the positive things, and accept the fact that unexpected problems will be waiting for you around every bend in the river. Focus your attention on the trees and nature and all the beauty surrounding you. Enjoy the moment.

List the ten most important things in your life; things you feel lucky to have.

- 1.
- 2.
- 3.
- 4.
- 5.
- 6.
- 7.
- 8.
- 9.
- 10.

*"Why take life so serious?*
*No one gets out alive."*

## Forks in the River

During your trip down the river you will be faced with many difficult decisions. While moving downstream in your raft, you will only be able to see what is directly ahead of you. Your decisions should always be based on what you can directly see. Do not try to predict what awaits you around the next bend, or what new obstacle you might encounter. To speculate will only serve to divert your focus. Do not expend unnecessary energy trying to predict the future. Savor the moment and enjoy the thrill of the ride. You must concentrate on the present direction of the river. This metaphor, of course, represents your journey through life; you must learn to live for today. Perhaps the most profound way to illustrate this philosophy is to share with you an ancient Sanskrit adage written over 3,000 years ago. Even today its wisdom is timeless.

"Each day well-lived makes every yesterday a memory of happiness and each tomorrow a vision of hope. Look well, therefore, to this one day, for it, and it alone is life."

Remember: a major part of life is overcoming difficulty. While cruising down the river, peacefully enjoying the ride, beware. You may encounter rapids or shallow waters. The only way to deal with these unexpected obstacles is to remain positive. Positive thinking fosters prudent decisions. Don't waste time with self-indulgent queries. "Why did this have to happen to me?" At times, your raft may capsize, and you will find yourself holding on for dear life, struggling to stay alive. Be aware that unwelcome events will frequently interfere with your voyage. It is nearly impossible to journey through life without turmoil. Accepting adversity and maintaining your composure will act as a life vest.

There will always be low points; periods when your raft is dragging bottom. One minute you're effortlessly cruising along, absorbed with the wonder of nature, enraptured by a chorus of song birds, mesmerized by a blazing sunset, and suddenly you find yourself in harm's way. Maybe you just got fired, or you're going through a divorce, or perhaps you lost a loved one. You're at a low point in your life, feeling as though life couldn't get any worse, desolate and alone, wondering how to overcome this formidable challenge. To survive you must evoke enormous levels of inner strength. You must carry your raft to higher waters. Take control and pull yourself together. Maintain a positive attitude by facing adversity head-on. Concentrate on your ultimate goal: reaching the Lake of Dreams.

> ### *"Adversity cause some men to break; others to break records."*
> **William A. Wardl**

## The Influence of Others

At times, as you negotiate your way down the river, you will have a firm grip on your objectives, feeling completely in control. You will be focused on your ultimate destiny, everything will appear to be great. You are concentrating on the present, all of your decisions are rational and based on the information at hand. Suddenly, you notice a group of people gathered at the shore, waving and encouraging you to join them. At first, you believe that their intentions are forthright, but beware. Not everyone will rejoice in your accomplishment. Not everyone will revel in your joy. There is an overly-used cliche' that summarizes this phenomenon poignantly: Misery loves company. You see, not all people subscribe to positive thinking, or follow their rivers to the Lake of Dreams. Many perversely enjoy wallowing in a pool of despair and discontent. And their lifelong ambition is to enlist as many followers as possible, because misery truly does love company. Watch out for those who seemingly appear to be advocates, yet conspire to sabotage your voyage.

Often, they will be cleverly disguised. Never, ever abandon your game plan. Even a temporary diversion can dramatically compromise your plan. Remember: you are in total control of your destiny. Live for the moment. Carpe diem.

# First Step Back

# Chapter Two: One Step Back Modern Man; the Search for Self Enlightenment

This chapter is designed to help you get in touch with your human instincts, traits that were inherent at birth, yet abandoned in your youth. "Modern Man" represents these instincts.

It is also my objective in this chapter to jump start your thinking and compel you to search for your own answers.

In geological terms, it wasn't too long ago that primitive man inhabited the earth and lived off the fruits and vegetables and grains provided by Mother Nature. As we evolved, we began to separate ourselves from the land. Archeologists have uncovered evidence to support the theory that Homo sapiens have walked this planet for over a million years. Primitive humans were great hunters and bonded closely with nature. They relied on their natural instincts to travel the continent in search for food and shelter. Modern man has been integrated into an industrial society, a dramatic departure from early man. Man's quest to conquer and expand is an ongoing process. Unfortunately, not all progress is productive. As we move forward with an industrial-driven society, we must replenish what we have destroyed. All indications suggest that we will continue to develop vacant land until it ceases to exit.

*"Only after the last tree has been cut down;*
*Only after the last fish has been caught;*
*Only after the last river has been poisoned;*
*Only then will you realize that money*
*cannot be eaten."*
**Cree Indian Prophecy**

Scientists believe that a major transformation of humankind took place during a period known as the Agricultural Era. Ancient tribes planted in the spring and harvested in the fall. As these tribes evolved from hunting to gathering, they began to form communities that fostered the birth of contemporary civilization. As the tribes settled as farmers, a more rigid social structure was needed. Temples and ceremonial centers were built, resulting in the need for a value system. During this agricultural transformation, humans also experienced a physiological metamorphosis. Many people of this era walked in the shaman. Shamanism is a primitive religion in which mediation between the visible and spirit world is effected by the shamans. Those who lived in the shaman renounced the traditional theory of life and searched for the unknown. They were people who lived in both the conscious and subconscious world. Their goal was not to seek answers, but to look for understanding. They were healers and travelers who were connected to the spirit of life. As humans evolved, their quest to conquer and build escalated, which promoted the rise of modern man and contemporary civilization, and the decline of ancient traditions.

A main characteristic of contemporary civilization is its ability to separate itself from nature. Unlike modern man, tribal farmers existed as one with nature. Separation from the fundamental philosophies of the tribal farmer to modern man's quest to industrialize the world has lead to the destruction of the Earth. For instance, humans are forced to build levees and damns to revitalize our poisoned rivers. Trees are being destroyed in great numbers, while the land and waters are polluted, and our air is intoxicated with gaseous poisons. In less than a decade, rain forests, a haven for hundreds of species of wildlife, all an integral component in the food chain, will vanish. Tribal farmers would have considered the singular act of cutting down even one tree as heinous as killing one's mother.

Our ambition to control the world, all of its inhabitants, and the environment, have caused a profoundly consequential result. Wars are waged without foresight or consideration for the effect on humankind. Our children have little or no understanding of their origin. People are born, live their lives, and die without ever truly understanding their purpose on Earth. Modern man has taken for granted those God-given instincts innate at birth.

I'd like to share a story with you about a bear cub. The story—a simple tale indeed—reveals the magical power of natural instincts. A young bear cub was separated from its mother and forced to live on his own. Although the cub had no idea how to survive in the wild without the nurturing and protection of his mother, he had inherited instincts that enabled him to develop those intrinsic skills. The cub knew—without ever being taught by his mother—that he needed to find water, hunt and capture prey, protect himself from enemies, and find suitable shelter. Under these adverse, less than ideal circumstances, the bear cub either had to enlist his instincts to survive or forfeit his life.

Humans share the same instincts to survive as animals, however, most of these instincts have been repressed. The only attribute that distinguishes humans from other animals is our faculty to reason and the conscious ability to make rational decisions. Humans are animals just like every other creature in the ecosystem. We are, of course, on top of the food chain, but all creatures share one characteristic: self-preservation. Ironically, our ability to reason, has in some respects become our nemesis. While global industrialization runs rampant, and modern man abandons his natural instincts to coexist with lesser animals and Mother Nature, we are destroying planet Earth in the wake of progress. We have arrogantly decided that the world belongs to us and its destiny is in our hands.

*Naked a man comes into the world and naked he leaves it, after all is said and done he leaves nothing except the good deeds he leaves behind."*
**Rashi**

It's never too late to change your perspective. I encourage you to look inside yourself for answers. Take two steps back, regress for just a moment. Allow your mind and body to live in harmony with the spirits of life. Integrate your subconscious with your conscious, and create one unit. Bond with nature once again and begin to experience the boundless miracles of life.

*"Vote with your life,*
*VOTE YES"*
**Das Enrgi**

## Intuition

Have you ever awakened and gone through your daily routine of getting ready with a secure feeling that nothing was out of the ordinary? But after rushing out the door you become overwhelmed with an unexplainable feeling that today you're going to get a speeding ticket? Most people tend to dismiss this phenomenon, until the dreaded flashing red lights appear in their rear view mirror and suddenly the premonition becomes a harsh and expensive reality. In retrospect of course, you feel like a fool. You knew it was going to happen, yet you did not take heed.

When you experience this kind of prodigy it is an inner vision. Your intuitive mind is speaking. Intuition communicates through signs, symbols, visions and even dreams. Almost everyone possesses some form of intuition. It is one of many natural instincts. This inner vision is your connection to the power of life. There are those supposed experts who discredit intuition, considering it to be merely coincidental. Granted, it is a most difficult phenomenon to study. Nonetheless, it is an integral part of the subconscious mind. Every day your mind is inundated with signals. Defining these signals and understanding their purpose is not an easy task.

On a number of occasions I have experienced the mystery and wonder of intuition. One such time stands out the most. When I was in my late teens, my friends and I were playing football one afternoon. There was nothing particularly unusual about this day, until the telephone rang. The minute I heard the ring, my intuitive instincts shifted into high gear. It was as if my nervous stomach was sending a message to my brain. Not only did I know that the call was from my girlfriend, but I also knew precisely what the conversation would be about.

"You won't believe what happened!" she almost yelled.

"You got in a wreck," I replied. It wasn't a question.

"Who told you?" she asked, sounding somewhat dumbfounded.

"Nobody."

I told her exactly what had happened. She pulled around a white Cutlass on the left side, thinking it was going to turn right. Suddenly, it turned left, directly into the side of my girlfriend's car.

"Good thing nobody got hurt," I added.

By now she was more annoyed than amused. "How did you know? I just got home. Did you see it happen? I can't believe you didn't stop and help!"

As you could imagine, I was incapable of explaining to my girlfriend what I had experienced. At the time, I wasn't sure myself. But that day marked an awakening in me, a profound hunger to understand the mystical power of life. You may never have experienced such an event, but even if your intuitive instincts are involuntarily repressed, you still possess the ability to see into the future.

Dreams are also inner visions that can give us meaningful insights into the future. They can also link us to our past. Sitting Bull, infamous Sioux leader who guided his people to victory against General George Custer's cavalry, was known to be a true shaman. In fact, shortly before he died, he claimed that his dreams were so clear he believed he could dream himself back into the world.

Think of your dreams as premonitions that give you insights into future events. In a dream state, time and space do not exist; you experience the moment. So the compelling question is: how do you tap into this enigmatic power regularly?

The first step is break down the wall of reality you have created in your mind. You must regress to a primitive state of mind and use your animal-like instincts inherited at birth. Do not search for scientific answers to understand these feelings. You must begin to trust and believe in your instincts. Trapping your attention is the next step. There is a clear distinction between focusing and trapping. Focusing requires conscious effort. You must "force" your mind to fix its attention on a subject. Trapping is more of an illusive state of nothingness. A period when your mind goes absolutely blank. You can provoke this dream-like state through the use of repetitive actions. For example, by chanting, drumming, or tapping a rock continuously, you can place your mind in a condition of dead space. In this state, you will be unable to remember what your mind was seeing or experiencing. When you allow your mind the freedom to be absorbed by this subconscious dream-state, you're utilizing the dominant power of subconscious mind control.

## Trusting Your Inner Vision

"The roller coaster of life will gradually become smoother when you learn to trust what your heart is telling you."

Déjà vu is another term for inner vision. The subconscious mind has experienced an event. But when the conscious mind experiences the same event, they connect. This connection evokes a peculiar feeling that you've already experienced something, but cannot remember when.

In order to unleash the power of this inner vision you must learn to trust your gut feelings. You cannot doubt or challenge your instincts.

However, it is important to thoroughly examine these inner visions to be certain they are not being misinterpreted. You may, at times, prematurely accept a vision as fact before allowing enough time for the full message to be received. Let me try to illustrate by telling a story.

Mary was a bright, single, thirty-year-old woman who had recently taken some measures to straighten out her life. Although marriage wasn't particularly appealing to her at this time, she was feeling the pressure of being thirty and single, and in desperate search of a boyfriend. To complicate things even more, her biological clock was ticking away. While on a business trip, she met a man who appeared to possess all that she was looking for in a mate. Their romance heated up quickly, and after dating for only a month, they rushed into marriage. Two years later they were divorced and Mary was right back where she started. She asked herself, "I wonder what happened?" To which she answered, "I must have bad intuitive skills."

Mary misread the message. Her heedless actions were clearly driven by emotions, not by her natural instincts. Fear caused Mary to be impetuous. Her desperate desire to find a mate distorted her ability to follow her intuition.

An inner vision can be misinterpreted by fear, anxiety, rejection and several other external factors. For example, suppose you were in need of a job and were on your way to an interview. A natural inclination would be to ask yourself, "Will I get the job?" You hope, of course, that the answer is, "Yes." However, if that little voice in your head says, "No," or worse yet, doesn't answer, you might plummet to a state of fear and negative thinking. Your body language will reflect those negative internal thoughts, and you may not get the job. It can almost be called a self-fulfilling prophecy. Don't allow your conscious mind to eclipse the subconscious mind. Be in tune with both your subconscious mind and your body.

> *"Man's mind, once stretched by a new idea, never regains its original dimensions."*
> **Oliver Wendell Holmes**

**The Sacred Silence - Finding the Vision**

You exist in duality; part flesh and part spirit. The spiritual mind, or the subconscious, is the purest part. Unfortunately, your conscious mind is used almost exclusively. To understand your inner visions and to gain insights into their importance, you must learn to rouse your spiritual mind. Due to lack of use, your spiritual mind has become weak. The more powerful your conscious mind, the weaker your spiritual mind. Your conscious mind is constantly being nourished. But in order to awaken your spiritual mind you must depart from traditional thinking.

After years of discontent and unfulfilled lives, many people search for answers through religion. Religion can act as a catalyst and lead you to the door, but only you can open it. A balance must exist between the conscious and subconscious mind. When the two coexist in harmony, your mind will be at peace.

If you imagined your mind as a body of water, what would you see? Think about everything you experience during a normal day: noisy traffic, deadlines, pressing financial obligations, hectic schedules, unreasonable bosses, screaming children. Would your body of water have violent waves crashing on the beach? To begin to understand the power of life, you must remove the counterproductive thoughts from your mind. Your body of water should be a quiet pond in a distant place. There are no ripples in the water, just a serene relaxing state of mind. Meditation is one of the best techniques to get you to this point.

> *"Accept the challenges, so that you may feel the exhilaration of victory"*
> **General George S. Patton**

## The Basic Fundamentals of Meditation

Meditation is a contemplative state of mind endorsed by many religions and philosophers. Meditation is defined as the act or process of thinking. It is believed that most people are incapable of using more than 10% of their brains. Some people use even less. Are there methods or exercises that will serve to awaken more of your brain? Yes, there are. Conventional wisdom might suggest that reading more books or studying more diligently would help to expand your brain. These methods will marginally help, but to maximize the use of your brain you must learn to meditate. Through meditation you can sustain a subconscious state of mind, which will allow you to utilize more of your brainpower. There are four fundamental keys to meditation.

The first is relaxation. For the meditation process to be successful, your body must be completely relaxed. You cannot force yourself to relax. The harder you try, the more difficult it becomes. Find a cozy place, free of all distractions. Perhaps a remote area in a park, or the wilderness, or even a quiet part of your home.

The second step is to find your comfort zone. If you do not maintain a comfortable position you will be distracted. For beginners, I suggest lying down. As you begin to master the techniques of meditation, you will be able to do it while talking, walking, or even while you are engaged in a strenuous activity. It's mind over matter. When you achieve a state of comfort and totally relax your mind, distractions will disappear as you become internally focused.

Have you ever seen a coal walker, a person who walks barefoot across burning coals? Contrary to what you might believe, this is not a trick. The coal walkers are able to transition into such a complete meditative state that they are able to walk across the coals without feeling discomfort. You, too, in a sense, can insulate yourself from all the "heat" in your life by learning to control your mind and body.

The third step is vitally important. Before attempting to meditate, you must maintain a peaceful, open minded attitude. One of the most common reasons for failure is trying too hard, forcing yourself to be tranquil. The most effective way to achieve a state of quietude is to concentrate on a focal point during the meditation process. Think, for example, of a calm pond. If your mind begins to wander, don't fight it, try to maintain a passive posture. If you begin to think about where your mind is wondering, you will give it the power to move further away. By remaining passive you are allowing your body and mind to wander effortlessly. As these distracting thoughts pass through your mind, you can then redirect your attention to the focal point.

The fourth step is to choose a location, a place that you will use exclusively for meditation. Condition your mind so that each time you go to this special place, you are there for only one reason. I would find a quiet, secluded area, free from all distractions. Once you are situated, begin by focusing on the calm pond. Think about the sounds of water. If you desire, play some relaxing music.

Reaching a point of complete meditation may, at first, be difficult. If you are a novice you may experience fierce internal struggles because you are embarking on a new, unfamiliar adventure. Often, a beginner may not be able to distinguish between meditating and dreaming. Dreaming is actually a part of the meditation process. When you sleep, your heart rate decreases dramatically. The same is true for meditation. Meditation is similar to the REM state of sleeping, when your dreams are the most active and easiest to recall.

## Guided Meditation Techniques

To reach this point of inner silence, find a partner who is also seeking personal enlightenment. Lie down on a hard surface or in the middle of the floor. Put on some soft music to prevent any background noise from distracting you. Place a blanket over yourself to keep you warm; your body temperature will decrease as your heart rate lowers. Do not cross your hands or feet. Lie absolutely flat, with your feet slightly turned outward, and your hands by your side, not touching your body. Your partner will be your guide, and lead you through a meditation. He or she should use a soft, friendly voice and remain quiet between instructions.

**Step 1:** Control your breathing. Inhale deeply. Hold your breath, then slowly exhale. Repeat this process, each time holding your breath a little longer, but not more than a minute. During this breathing exercise your focal point should be on inhaling and exhaling.

**Step 2:** The guide should monitor this breathing exercise, helping the meditator to take deeper breaths, and hold them longer before exhaling. Take another breath and imagine all the tension in your body filling your lungs as you inhale. When you exhale, feel all the tension escape from your body as the air passes your lips. Continue for three to five breaths. Your focal point is to feel the tension being released.

**Step 3:** Calming the Body. You are now going to change the focal point from breathing to your body. Begin with your arms. As you inhale, tighten the arm muscles as much as possible, flexing the muscles and holding it. As you exhale to release the tension, allow your arms to relax. Your guide will instruct you to do this with your legs, stomach, shoulders, back, neck, and head. Be certain that you perform this exercise on every muscle group in your body, but always finish with your head. In this process, move your focal point to whichever part of your body is being flexed. Continue to release tension as you exhale. The controlled breathing, combined with the release of tension, will result in a deeper level of relaxation. If a certain body part is particularly stubborn and refuses to relax, continue until it cooperates. Each time you relax a body part it should feel "heavy," as if it were actually sinking into the floor.

**Step 4.** The White Light. The guide will instruct you to imagine a beam of white light shooting from the sky and entering your body. The light beam will continue through the body in the same sequence in which you relaxed your body in Step 3. If you started with your arms, imagine the light entering through your fingertips. The guide should speak in a soothing, calming, relaxing manner. The focal point should be directed to the body part through which the light is currently entering. If it entered through your finger tips, imagine it traveling through your arm toward your shoulder. The guide should describe the warm sensation you will feel as the light passes through the body.

**Step 5.** The gravitational pull. The guide now instructs you to feel the weight of each body part being pulled into the ground. Again, do this in the same sequence as Step 3. As each body part is focused on, you should feel as if it is being disconnected from the skeletal system. The focal point is directed to the body part being pulled to the ground.

**Step 6.** Now that you have completed the relaxation process for the body, it is time to focus on your mind. Lying there, completely relaxed, imagine your body levitating off the ground, as if it were flying. Your guide will ask you to imagine your body becoming lighter and lighter as it floats off the ground. The focal point is your body lifting off the ground. Fly with the sound of the background music. Do this for approximately one minute.

**Step 7.** To land, the guide will bring you back to the surface by asking you to take a deep breath and hold it, then exhale. This will release all the tension in your mind. The guide will now bring you back to full consciousness by instructing you to move your feet, hands, and so forth. This meditation exercise might make you somewhat dizzy, so I strongly advise you to wait a few minutes before standing.

Now that you have completed the process, you should practice regularly. After four or five sessions you should reach a point where you can complete the meditation exercise without the assistance of a guide. The key is to always have a focal point. Remember the four fundamentals of meditation: relaxation, comfort, receptive attitude, and having a focal point. How do you know when you are successfully meditating? When your mind is at total peace, like the quiet pond.

## "Your Mind should be as calm as a pond on a quiet summer day."

## Getting Back in Touch

We are born into an unfamiliar world, an artificial environment. Bright lamps, sophisticated machines, doctors, and nurses surround us the moment we draw our first breath. Our parents, thrilled to have accomplished one of life's most fulfilling ambitions, are anxious to take us home. We are their prize; a symbol of their love. From the moment we are born, we begin to learn about the world and develop our personalities as we respond to our new surroundings. It is believed that the learning process actually begins in the womb.

During the first few months of infancy, most parents spend a great deal of time teaching and entertaining their children. Unfortunately, due to financial pressures, many parents are forced to place their children in day care facilities, where, more often than not, the children do not receive the same attention or nurturing they would have from their parents. As they grow older, this quality time begins to decline.  By the time a child reaches his or her teenage years, the parents and child have almost completely lost their connection. Consequently, the children become more influenced by teachers, daycare providers, and their peers than by their parents.  Over the years, this disconnection from a traditional family structure can result in troubled children.

Children, by virtue of an inherent curiosity, are intrigued by everything around them.  They possess a particular affinity for animals and nature, awestruck by the wonder of God's creatures and Mother Nature's magic.  We often look back at ourselves as youngsters and remember all the carefree, impulsive things we did, without guilt and without forethought. Running through lawn sprinklers on a hot summer day, climbing a tree, riding our bikes down to the nearest creek and capturing turtles. We were all engrossed with the outdoors, wanting to feel, see, smell, touch and hear all that we could.  We did not understand this desire at the time, but what we were experiencing was the gift of life; the power of existence.

For some unknown reason many children abandon their inclination to bond with nature and begin to spend far too much time in front of the television or playing video games.  These are artificial stimuli that tend to curb their desire for action and excitement.  Learning about life as a participant is replaced with watching it as a spectator through characters on television programs.  One can only experience the power of life by participating in the event first hand.  Those who live life to the fullest, making every minute an adventure, do not need to live vicariously through television characters. Think of your own life as a movie. As a child all you really cared about was getting your chores done so you could go outside and play. Remember how sad you were on rainy days when you couldn't go outside? The moment the rain stopped, you would run outside, hoping to get a glimpse of a rainbow. I remember days like this as if they were yesterday. How many of us would trade our adult lives, with all the stress and pressure and responsibilities, for the chance to be a child again?

For most of us, our parents were instrumental in teaching us how to become productive, successful adults. But how many taught us to live a life full of adventure? It is possible to go through life feeling the same carefree joy you did as a child. But it was not our parent's responsibility to lead the way. We are not victims. We are the architects of our own destiny. Growing up does not mean to abandon those things we so enjoyed as children; it means to take full responsibility for our lives without laying blame or making excuses.

> *"The quality of a person's life is in direct proportion to their commitment to excellence, regardless of their chosen field of endeavor."*
> **Vincent T. Lombardi**

When you go through life trying to fit a role, you lose your personality and degrade your quality of life. I attended a party one night and overheard this couple talking about work.  The husband explained that he goes to work at seven a.m. and often works until eleven p.m., a fourteen hour work day.  I thought to myself, "How much fun is that?"  He justified this insanity by explaining that the company for whom he worked relied on him to secure contracts that require this much effort.

"What about life?" I asked him.

He said that he'd been working these hours for three months.  The man, proud as could be, sounded as if he deserved a medal.  I was amazed.  His wife, remarkably, was equally excited with her husband's success.

I shook my head and said, "That's really amazing.  I try to work as little as possible."

They looked at me, obviously taken aback. I didn't say another word, hoping it would sink in.

## Shaped and Modeled to Conform

Think back to the days when you were in grade school.  Remember having to raise your hand and ask permission to use the rest room?  You even had to have a pass just to walk in the halls.  You were also required to raise your hand if you wanted to speak.  And if unanticipated family problems prevented you from completing your required homework, you still got reprimanded without a valid excuse from your parents.  School, in general, teaches children how to conform to the rules of society in hopes that this will result in productive adults.  Teachers train children to develop personalities that do not go against the grain of acceptable behavior.  The majority of us fit into this role rather conveniently. What about the nonconformists, those whose personalities clash with authority? Schools frequently employ methods to alter these personalities so they will integrate well with others. By processing children and attempting to alter their personalities, educators may be limiting their capacity to learn. When a child reacts to a natural instinct and is punished, these children begin to question their judgements. Ultimately, they suppress their natural behavior. This oppression erodes the child's level of confidence and causes greater problems in later years.

## Kyle

Not too long ago I was scheduled to speak before a group of seventh-graders. I thought it would be a good idea to telephone the teacher ahead of time, just to get a brief overview of the agenda. Quite to my dismay, rather than discuss the agenda, she repeatedly warned me to beware of a student named Kyle. She explained in great detail, and with noticeable anxiety, that Kyle would, undoubtedly, disrupt my lecture like he'd done so many times before. She claimed that he was her most difficult student, and that he had a chronic behavioral problem. She even went on to say that she would be absolutely thrilled if Kyle weren't in her class. I wondered just how bad this kid could be to make his teacher so resigned.

The next day when I arrived at school, I was excited to meet Kyle. Unlike his teacher, who seemed to have given up on him, I guessed that there was something special about this kid.  When Kyle walked in the door I spotted him immediately. I inconspicuously watched him find his chair. The bell rang and I introduced my partner and myself, then I began to talk.  Kyle raised his hand several times and asked some interesting questions.  The teacher shook her head in disgust.  She didn't like Kyle, I surmised, because his conduct did not embody a personality compatible with the other students.  Children like Kyle are often forced to bury their creative emotions, causing them to escape from reality.  Aren't we all in search of who we really are?  Don't we all wish to uncover our true personalities?

So, the theme of this chapter is a simple, yet profound one: get back in touch with your natural instincts.  Taking this first important step back will put you in touch with your subconscious state of mind.  Through the methods of meditation you will uncover your true identity, and never again will you be forced to conform to a lifestyle inconsistent with who you really are.

**_Style is knowing who you are, what you want to say, and not giving a damn._**
**_Gore Vidal_**

# Second Step Back

# The Wheel of Emotions

**Fear • Anger • Jealousy • Loneliness • Hatred**

Negative

YOU

Positive

**Love • Hope • Faith • Courage • Enthusiasm**

# Chapter Three:
## The Mirror Never Lies

I have always believed that you can read a person merely by observing their accomplishments in life or by noting what they are trying to avoid. We all share one common bond: the ability to feel physical and emotional pain.

With few exceptions, human beings harbor emotional scars. It makes little difference whether they're rich, poor, overweight, slender, African-American, Caucasian, intelligent or mentally challenged, just about every person walking the planet has open wounds that need to be healed. Even families that outwardly appear to be well-adjusted have their share of difficulties. We all have secret hiding places for those unpleasant memories we so conveniently stow away in our subconscious mind. Many are buried so deeply our conscious mind is unaware that they even exist. Whether we are awake or asleep, these ominous memories—no matter how securely repressed—affect our behavior and actions. You cannot arbitrarily dismiss this pain. You must first thoroughly accept that it actually happened by investigating the how or why, and to what extent it affected your life. You can reprogram your mind and your behavior by facing the pain head-on, and releasing it. This is a delicate matter because many of us have survived the pain and adapted quite well. Consider this a journey of the mind; an attempt to achieve greater self-enlightenment. The clearer your understanding of yourself, the more enriched your life will be. The answers you seek live in your soul, restlessly waiting to be discovered.

## The Wheel of Emotions

The wheel of emotions is a practical way for you to understand negative and positive behaviors. Every emotion is represented by a spoke. The links are the people in your life who have had the most influence on your behavior.

### The Spokes: Links to Emotions

- Family
- Friends
- Teachers/Educators
- Relatives
- Outside Influences

You are the center hub and all of the spokes revolve around you. Your spokes connect you to the wheel, which represents whatever emotion you're feeling. Each spoke can be either a positive or negative relationship; both in some cases. Positive and negative emotions are embedded into your subconscious mind.    At any particular moment you can elicit sufficient evidence to prove that your life is either miserable, depressing and out of control, or exciting, fulfilling, and cheerful. How these five links are connected to you is what determines the feeling you are experiencing.

> *"If we could hang all our sorrows on pegs*
> *and were allowed to pick those we liked*
> *best, each one of us would take back*
> *their own, for all the others would be*
> *even more difficult to bear."*
> **Reb Nahum**

### The Five Major Negative Emotions

**FEAR:**  Fear results from your inability to predict what's going to happen, therefore you are uncertain of the outcome.   How many times have you feared an impending event, only to discover that your anxiety was unfounded?    Rarely are outcomes as devastating as you anticipate.  Fear can be replaced with faith and a positive outlook. Always see the glass as half-full; never half-empty.

**ANGER:**    Anger impairs your ability to make logical decisions.   It is an unbridled, non-productive emotion that can be harnessed and controlled with practice.   Try to recognize what events or circumstances precipitate your anger. To be forewarned is to be forearmed.  When you begin to feel the early signs that anger is taking over, try to remove yourself from the situation before it gets out of hand.

**JEALOUSY:** This emotion is normally the result of low self-esteem or a lack of confidence. To some degree, even well-adjusted people deal with jealousy from time to time.

**LONELINESS:** We all, at some point in our lives, have felt alone. Even when surrounded by friends or involved in a romantic relationship, most people experienced loneliness. The more intimate friendships you cultivate, and the more time you expend interacting with people in a productive, mutually beneficial manner, the less likely you'll feel lonely.

**HATRED:** This vile emotion can do nothing but wreak havoc in your life. Ironically, it takes so much effort to hate, that it is remarkably easier to forgive. By understanding the motivation of those you resent, it may be possible for you to manage your feelings and to forgive. Remember: hatred does not directly hurt the person you hate. It does, however, consume and control you.

These negative emotions dramatically impact your life by distorting your personality and causing pain. There are those who think they can cleverly dismiss these emotions by denying that they truly exist. Some of the most insensitive, hardened individuals endure the most pain, even though outwardly they appear to be in control. They have conditioned their minds and bodies not to respond. Their subconscious mind, however, will always seek the truth. On the surface they appear to be fine, but inside they are enduring profound pain with no place to release it. These lost souls are torn between what they are trying to be and what they have become. Their behavior and outlook on life are hopeless. You have the choice to either ride a wave of positive emotions, or to allow negative emotions to rule your world. Only you can decide.

> *"Identifying your pain—is the first step in healing the soul."*

## The Five Major Positive Emotions

**LOVE:**   The words, "I Love You" are three tiny words, yet their magical power can heal even the most damaged heart.  To love another—whether romantic love, family love, or friendship love—is not the result of random circumstance or an accident of nature; it is a conscious choice.  The most wondrous thing about love is that one's capacity to love is limitless; you cannot deplete your supply.   In fact, the more you give, the greater your wellspring of love.   Only you can determine how much love you wish to have in your life.  When you act in a loving way, either toward yourself or others, the feeling perpetuates itself. "Learning to love yourself is the greatest love of all." It may also be the most mysterious aspect of love.  You cannot share your love without first loving yourself.   And to love yourself does not suggest that you are egocentric or conceited. Loving yourself paves the way for you to share your love with others, without restriction or limitation.

**HOPE:**  Hope helps you to maintain a tranquil, positive outlook on life, even during times of utter desolation.  Hope is the light at the end of a long, dark tunnel.  It is a safe path to peace of mind.  When you are faced with seemingly insurmountable obstacles, hope enables you to cope with these hardships and helps you to utilize your inner powers.  Hope is believing in yourself.

**FAITH:**  Without faith there would never be miracles.  Without miracles, life would be unremarkable.  Having faith is believing that all outcomes will be favorable and that anything is possible.

**COURAGE:**  Courage is driven by sheer will and determination.  It is the ability to stand and fight for what you believe, even when others criticize and ridicule you.  Martin Luther King III, one of the most courageous men in history, forfeited his life for his beliefs.  To die for what you believe is the most profound example of courage.  But through Doctor King's death, many of his dreams have been fulfilled through the efforts of others who benefitted from his courage.

**ENTHUSIASM:**  Enthusiasm is the emotion by which your aspirations become conceivable.  It is the engine that propels your ideas forward.  With enthusiasm you can achieve your most ambitious goals.  One of the most powerful merits of enthusiasm is that it is contagious and can positively affect everyone around you.

To lead a more fulfilling, productive life, you must learn to harness the awesome power of these positive emotions and incorporate them into your daily thought process. This is a formidable task, and it takes a great deal of perseverance. Negative thoughts will creep into your head and try to overpower you because it is much easier to be a pessimist than an optimist. Negative emotions, by virtue of their popularity among the masses, are insidious. They spread through the air like viruses, waiting to attack your immune system. Often, before you have a chance to defend yourself, negative emotions infect you. By the time you realize you've contracted a "disease," it's too late.

> *"No man chooses evil because it is evil;*
> *he only mistakes it for happiness, it's*
> *the good he seeks."*
> **Mary Wollstonecraft Shelley**

## Ways to Overcome Negative Thought

**1.** Ignore the couriers of bad news. The world is overrun with messengers of gloom because misery truly does love company. Do not give "negative crusaders" the opportunity to download negative thoughts. Example: I had a friend who would regularly visit me and incessantly complain about his troubled life. He wasn't seeking solutions to his problems; he preferred to wallow in his despair, and was hoping I would join his crusade by offering my own dismal exposé. Uninterested in participating in this unproductive campaign, I discovered a method to stop his assault. Every time he said something negative, I ignored him without comment. But when he said anything positive, I would reply with a lengthy response. After a while I conditioned him to keep our conversations positive and uplifting.

**2.** Although it is much easier said than done, look for a benefit in even the most negative situation. When you look at things "linearly," you can only see things one way. Try to view things "laterally." In other words, don't look at the obvious and dismiss any possibility that a situation can be interpreted in a more auspicious manner. Every circumstance—no matter how hopeless—can result in a favorable outcome. Back in the early nineties, Dale Franklin was a successful sales representative for a large software company. Sales were faltering, so one day Dale's boss called him to his office and announced, "We're going to have to let you go." Dale, as you might imagine, was devastated. He had a hefty mortgage payment and was responsible to provide for his family. Rather than pursuing another position selling software, Dale reluctantly accepted a position as an insurance salesman, believing this to be a temporary situation. Ten years later Dale was running the insurance company and earning more money in one year than he would have made in a decade selling software. Always look for "a diamond in the rough."

**3.** This may sound a bit cliché, but smile and the world smiles with you; cry and you cry alone. No matter what's going on in your life, keep flashing those pearly-whites!  Negative emotions will have a difficult time ruining your day when your smiling—it's your best self-defense mechanism. And the best part is that it doesn't cost you a penny to smile.  In fact, when you see other people positively responding to your happy face, negative emotions don't have a chance.

**4.**  When a negative thought invades your mind, don't give it time to fester.  Immediately recognize that its only purpose is to torment you and force it out of your mind by focusing on a happy thought.  Even if you have to literally scream it out of your head, get rid of it!

**5.**  Replace negative thoughts with positive ideas. Because ideas generally are more complex than negative thoughts, and require greater concentration, focus your attention on productive ideas and the negative thoughts will magically disappear.

### Making the Link—American Class Family

In 1997, I was speaking to an At-Risk class in an upper middle school in Texas.  These were a group of kids who were either potential drop outs or children with troubled families.  I had noticed that one of the students, Derrick, had not been in class the last three times I had visited.  Somewhat curious, I asked Derrick's teacher if he was ill, moved or perhaps dropped out of school.  The teacher, overtly agitated, sighed deeply and said,

"Derrick was suspended again for fighting and being disruptive." This puzzled me. Derrick was an average, happy-go-lucky kid. The teacher continued, "It just doesn't make sense. I met both his parents at a student teacher's meeting and they appeared to be a well-adjusted family. His dad has a great job, and his sister is in one of my other classes and she's doing just fine." After quizzing the teacher for a few minutes I learned a little about Derrick and his family. They were a typical upper-middle class family. Dad worked hard as a senior executive, and although like most families they had their share of problems, the family structure suggested stability. In spite of the seemingly productive household, Derrick had been suspended three times that year for arguing with teachers and fighting with other students. I knew there was more to the story. Why would an average student display such hostile behavior?

When he came back to class the following week, I sat with him and asked, "What's been bothering you, Derrick?"

His response didn't surprise me. "Everything is fine," he said. "What makes you think something's wrong?"

"Getting suspended three times for fighting doesn't sound fine to me," I said. "What's getting you so mad? Are other students picking on you?"

"No," he answered. "When someone won't listen to me or says something about me, I fly off the handle and hit them. I don't know why."

"Do you get along with your parents?" I asked. I could see his face tense.

"They're always on me about my grades and stuff."

I was reluctant to ask this question, but knew its answer was significant. "When your dad gets angry with you, does he yell or hit you?"

After a long silence he glanced at me with teary eyes and whispered, "Yes."

I've never professed to be an expert child psychologist, however, I didn't need an advanced degree in child behavior to understand Derrick's belligerent conduct. Externally, this family appeared to be normal. Mom and dad were still together, dad provided for his family, Derrick's sister was doing fine—how many families do you know like this? Outwardly, everything looks rosy. The problem is that from our perspective everything seems to be going fine. The son was a little too cantankerous, but more than likely he'd grow out of it. Right? Perhaps not.

I suspected that behind the scenes this family was not so normal. If I applied the wheel of positive and negative emotions I might have been able to analyze Derrick's behavior and unlock the mystery of his violent outbursts. The investigation began by finding the spoke or link to his behavior.

After the color returned to Derrick's face, I continued with my query. "What did your father do when you got suspended?"

Derrick was fidgeting in his chair. "Well . . . he hit me, pushed me, and told me if it happened again I wouldn't be able to walk." Derrick added that his father's temper was often out of control. Through further questioning, Derrick reluctantly confessed that often, in a fit of rage, his father had emotionally and physically abused Derrick's sister and mother as well.    It was now clear that Derrick's father had unresolved issues, perhaps from his own childhood, to deal with.    His unacceptable behavior was being imitated by his son.  There was also the distinct possibility that Derrick's grandfather was a violent man.

After talking a little more, and probing a lot less, I proposed to Derrick that he had only three clear choices:

**1)**  He could ignore his destructive behavior, dismiss it as a temporary state of being, which would result in Derrick one day acting like his father, or quite possibly becoming even more hostile and abusive. This, I suggested, was not a wise choice.

**2)**  He could acknowledge his dysfunctional behavior and make a promise to himself not to follow in his father's footsteps. I told Derrick that this could be a solution.   However, I cautioned him.  He might be able to deal with one aspect of his problem, which to me was very complex, but few people can successfully tackle such a formidable problem on their own.

**3)** The last option truly was Derrick's only option. To more clearly understand and deal with those demons controlling Derrick's behavior, he needed to reach out for help.  I suggested that he seek counseling, or at a minimum, read several self-help books that would give him some perspective on how to deal with his problems.

*"If you're too scared to admit you're hurting;
don't be upset when others don't care."*

## Making the Link: The Negative and Positive Emotional Wheel

Hopefully, you were able to make a connection with the family described above by understanding that the violence was a negative emotion linked to the father. As with any wheel, it goes around and never changes its momentum until someone or some thing disrupts its normal pattern. Remember: In your life, you are the hub of this wheel, and the spokes connect you to both positive and negative emotions. The spokes represent the people who play a significant role in your life, both past and present. A negative emotion results in a broken spoke. To repair the spoke, you must first identify who it represents, and then "fix" it by employing the healing methods explained later in this chapter. The wheel can still spin with broken spokes, but not as efficiently as it should. Each negative emotion slows the wheel's motion; too many broken spokes will destroy the wheel permanently.

Derrick, the young man in the story, had to explore his father's past to identify the link. Gathering information from relatives and friends of the family, learning everything possible about his parents, was an integral part of Derrick's healing. The greater his exploration into his families' characteristics, the clearer he would begin to understand his own behavioral traits and personality.

There are several thought provoking theories about the generation Derrick's parents were born into that might help explain why and how negative emotions are "handed down." During this generation past, family matters were not common knowledge; problems remained inside the home. Physical punishment such as spankings and belt whippings were common. In fact, hitting your children in general was considered an acceptable reprimand. Today, if you strike your child, there's a good chance you'll end up in front of a judge.

These were difficult times for many Americans. Unlike today, with big screen televisions, sophisticated computer systems, and everyone sporting cellular telephones, money was scarce, and secure, well-paying jobs were hard to come by. And for the most part, women were homemakers and did not financially contribute to the household. If you carefully examine the lifestyle of your great grandparents, you might be shocked to learn that a woman's role in the home was as a subservient housekeeper. The husband was a self-proclaimed "King of the Castle," and he ruled his home with a firm hand. This environment did not promote democracy, or independent thinking. In this male-dominated society, women were not even allowed to vote!

By carefully analyzing the history of man and his behavioral patterns, you will begin to see how this egocentric attitude from generations past can still affect a young man's life even today. Needless to say, life today—although stressful—has certainly gotten better. By regressing and analyzing your past, you, just like Derrick can begin to understand your own wheel of emotions, repair the broken spokes, and release the pain you've been holding inside.   When you make a conscious decision to unlock the mysteries of your past, and examine the reasons for your everyday struggles, your life will take on a new, fulfilling direction.

Through additional queries, I learned that Derrick's father, quite remarkably, was a kind man, and loved his family dearly.  But when times were rough, uncontrollable anger emerged and took over.   After the outburst, he felt horrible inside and wished he hadn't exploded.  But then, of course, it was too late.  His problem stemmed from an inability to express his adverse feelings to his family and finding ways to relieve them without physical violence.  This type of behavior often progresses from one generation to another. The children witness their parent's rage and begin to imitate this conduct.  If they are not taught how to deal with and control their anger, more than likely they will become just as abusive.

The only effective way to heal a wound or harness a negative emotion such as this is to determine who represents the root of the problem, and talk to them in a pro-active, non-confrontational manner.  You must exercise the utmost discretion and civility when approaching this person.  More than likely they have buried the pain and don't want to discuss it.  Quite possibly it may be locked in their subconscious.  If you are unsuccessful in initiating a productive, mutually beneficial conversation, move on with your life and begin the process of creating new spokes in your wheel.

*"Except the challenges so that you may feel the exhilaration of victory."*

## Recreating the Wheel

Begin the cleansing process by first locating a quiet room in your home, free from all distractions. No telephone interruptions, television, or background music. Instead of using conventional lighting, light a candle. Make yourself comfortable. Have some paper and a pen handy. Sit upright, remain conscious of your posture, and begin to regulate your breathing just like you might when meditating. Relax your body and ease your mind. What you're trying to achieve is a state of tranquility and inner peace. Now begin to evaluate your behavior, exploring aspects of your conduct that have been troubling you. Discover which spoke has caused you pain. Once you have found it, ask yourself, "What could I have done differently to have changed the outcome? Was it my fault? What were the circumstances that caused me to act this way?"

More often than not, you were a victim of someone else's pain. They imposed this pain on you because of their inability to deal with it. This is the moment of truth; it is time to face these demons head-on and slay them. You cannot overcome them until you fully explore the reasons and understand the circumstances associated with their existence. Don't expect that a lifetime of pain can be released instantly. If you are overwhelmed with emotion, let it go. Remember that crying is an important part of the healing process. Scream or curse, whatever is necessary to release the pain through some form of physical recognition. Now it's time to use the paper and pen.

**Sequence of Events.** Write a detailed account of the events that resulted in your pain. Write this in third person, which will help maintain your objectivity. You may only remember the events that didn't hurt, but you must force yourself to recreate all of the hurtful details. Assume the role as an investigative reporter, as if you were writing about someone else.

**Identify the Problem.** In first person, outline how this has affected your life. What do you fear? How does it make you feel when you think about it? How did this event affect others?

**Letting Go and Cleansing the Soul.** Write a letter to the person who hurt you, or to the person you hurt. This is a confession. Tell the whole story, no matter how difficult. Explain in great detail how this has negatively affected your life. If someone else is responsible for the pain, forgive them. If you are accountable, apologize.

**Moving Forward.** Now it is time to create your future. You are without limitation or boundaries. Outline your plan for the future and explain how this experience is going to make a positive difference in your life and for those people fortunate enough to know you. This is the most important part of the healing process. Make a commitment to yourself that you will never again walk down this dark path. Remember: There are no victims in this world, only volunteers.

When the story is completed, it's now time for you to read it aloud. Not once, but over and over, until the words are forever etched in your mind. It's going to hurt, but for the first time in your life it will be a good hurt. After you have read it, fold it neatly and put it in your back pocket. Carry it with you for three days. Read it often. Keeping it with you at all times will ultimately send a symbolic message to your conscious mind that you have confronted this horrible secret, faced the pain head-on, and successfully slain the demon. Perhaps you may need more than three days. Whatever it takes. When the pain is finally gone, read the story one more time. When you're finished, put a match to it and watch it burn with a smile on your face. Whisper to yourself:

"My pain is gone forever. It will never control me again. I forgive myself and everyone else involved. I am healed and this is a turning point in my life. I have absolved myself of fear and my future is mine to control. I am the captain of my own ship."

*"When someone hurts your feelings,*
*it's unimportant unless you persist in*
*remembering it."*

# A Lifetime Forward

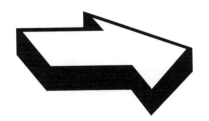

# Planting a Commitment Tree

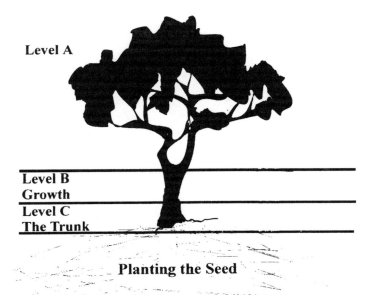

Level A

Level B
Growth

Level C
The Trunk

Planting the Seed

Level D
The Roots

# Chapter Four:
## The Commitment Tree;
## Planting a Tree that will Bear Fruit

A goal is defined as: the purpose toward which an endeavor is directed; an objective. It is something we wish to accomplish or a target we are trying to reach. Since early childhood, most of us have been taught to set goals and work hard to reach them. Although setting goals may at first appear to be wise, I feel that they can often lead to unfulfilled objectives. To "hope" and "intend" are words synonomus with goal setting. These are vague words, almost passive. And they do not evoke enough resolve to convert goals into reality. Almost everyone has established goals, but most people lack a workable game plan to achieve these goals and make them part of their lives. Typically, when you set goals they are usually linked to a start date. Case in point: how many people make New Year's resolutions? Why do we wait until the beginning of the year to change a part of our behavior that we know should have been altered long ago?  How many people truly live up to their New Year's resolutions?

Michael Jenkins was a grossly overweight sales manager working in the paper industry.  Tipping the scales at three-hundred-fifty pounds and standing only five-foot-eight, Jenkins was a prime candiate for fatal health problems.  While visiting his family doctor for chest pains, the doctor, concerned with Jenkins high cholestoral level and his one-hundred-pound weight gain since his last visit, insisted that Jenkins lose one-hundred-twenty-five pounds.  Jenkins had been struggling with a weight problem for over three years, and this was not the first time his doctor had suggested that Jenkins lose weight.  At each visit the doctor warned Jenkins that if he didn't change his eating habits, quite smoking and drinking, and lose a significant amount of weight, Jenkins could die.  Everytime the doctor issued this warning, Jenkins would offer the same reply, "It's my New Year's resolution, Doc."  It was only September and the doctor cautioned that Jenkins needed to act immediately.  What could possibly have been a more compelling motivator than announcing to a patient that he could die at any moment?

On January first, Jenkins lived up to his promise.  He reduced the fat and calories in his diet, became more active, and remarkably lost fifty-four pounds in three months.  This accomplishment might have proven to be an event to celebrate, but unfortunalety, Micheal Jenkins ran out of time in October and died of a heart attack at the age of 45.  Yes, he was committed to his resolution, but it was just too little, too late.

When we decide that a particular change is necessary in our lives, why do we postpone it until the beginning of the year, or some other insignificant benchmark?  To procrastinate any change that will enrich our lives and make us healthier, happier, or more fulfilled is illogical.  But we are humans and human nature dictates much of what we do.  Our inactions don't always conform to rational thinking.  Perhaps we require a period of time to "digest" the affect of this change, or we need to carefully consider the consequence of failure.  By postponing what we know should be changed immediately, we set the stage for failure.  Life continues and our new goals and resolutions may not fit into our life style, so they remain on the drawing board.  There is a solution.  Instead of setting goals and resolutions, use a concept I call, "making commitments."  A commitment is a promise, a pledge to achieve an objective within a specific time period.  The distinction between a goal and a commitment is a solemn oath.

> *"The people who get on in this world*
> *are the people who get up and look for*
> *the circumstances they want, and,*
> *if they can't find  them, make them."*
> **George Bernard Shaw**

Being committed to a particular objective requires conviction.  Unlike a goal, when you tend to change direction at the first sign of difficulty, a commitment is a covenant from which you cannot and will not release yourself, even at times of supreme tribulation. Goals can be changed, altered, and modified to make them more convenient. A commitment is a formal contract, witnessed and underwritten by your integrity. It is a willingness to do whatever is required to get what you want.

When I began my career in the business world, I set a goal to make five-thousand-dollars a month. Every day I would work hard toward achieving this magic number. Often I would make additional sales calls and many days I worked long hours. Some months I would reach my earning objective, and enjoy an inexplicable feeling of euphoria. Other months I would fall short and feel like a failure. From one day to the next, I rode an emotional roller coaster. I began to second-guess myself, questioning my ability. Whether I reached my goal or not, there was never truly a peaceful feeling. Every day I asked the same haunting questions: "Could I have worked harder? What could I have done differently?"

For quite some time, the whole concept of goal setting bothered me. I knew that there had to be a better way to reach my objectives without being subjected to so much anxiety. I decided—instead of continuing with my goal—to make a commitment to start and operate my own business. I did not set a financial objective or confine myself to a specific timeline, but I did commit to make a great deal of money. I had total conviction to make my vision a reality. I altered my mindset and consructed a written, detailed plan of how I would achieve this objective. Every day I planned my work and worked my plan, without feeling self-imposed pressure or stress. Failure was not an option.  I was committed to reach my objective and had devised a step by step plan that enabled me to achieve it.

So, think about your goals.  Are they vague? Do they rely on "hope" and "intention?"  Do you have a written plan?  Are you experiencing stress and anxiety because these goals continue to outdistance you?  Do you modify your goals so they conform to your daily lifestyle?  What is it that you truly want to accomplish?  In writing, outline your objectives.  Devise a step by step plan to reach these objectives.   Now, make a commitment to yourself that you will diligently follow this plan.  Remember: if your objective isn't in writing, it's only a goal.

I have always been fascinated with the rationale people employ to choose a particular profession.   What factors influenced their decision?  What compelled them to start a given type of business?   To me, exploring this phenonenon is extremely thought provoking.  The reasons why and the stories associated with these vocational preferences intrigue me. In many cases, it is easy to see how people failed.  On the other hand, it's not difficult to understand how successful people had the conviction to stay with their chosen field, even at times of severe difficulty.  As I began to investigate, I learned that many professions yielded fulfillment, happiness and prosperity.   Lawyers, doctors, musicians, actors, program designers, salespeople, consultants, brokers, manufacturers, people from all walks of life have reached admirable levels of wealth and personal greatness. Although each successful person had a different level of drive and ambition, the one common thread that united them was that each of them followed their game plan. This does not suggest that certain modifications were not required as economic conditions changed, but they never waivered from their overall objectives.

In 1948, Charles Lazarus followed through with a longtime idea and opened a children's furniture store in Washignton D.C. His dream was to provide familes with quality merchandise at everyday low prices. As his vison became reality and his client base developed, he diversified his operation by offering toys as well as cribs, playpens, and other pieces of furniture. Through his tireless efforts and unwavering commitment to achieve his objective, he amassed a solid foundation of loyal customers who patronized his store regularly. In less than three years, Lazarus opened three more stores, one of which was twenty-five-thousand square feet. He had developed a refreshing new concept in retailing: the toy superstore. Today there are over eight-hundred-eleven Toys R Us stores worldwide, with annual sales exceeding six-billion dollars. Although Lazarus may have altered his plan as needed because of unforeseen circumstances, he never abandoned his original commitment.

**"Today's opportunities erase
yesterday's failures."**
**Gene Brown**

## Plant a Commitment Tree

To begin to plant a commitment tree I want you to write down what it is that you are committing yourself to become. For example, to become a great parent, successful business person, or to become rich. Whatever the idea, it is "your seed." To plant your seed you have visualize yourself obtaining this objective. Charles Lazarus seed was opening a childrens store. Think about what your life will be like in twenty years and how this commitment will change your life from where you are today.

Once the seed has been planted you have to develop a game plan that will allow your commitment to grow and become strong. Developing your roots means getting the necessary education and training. Adjusting your lifestyle to accommodate this commitment. Do all the neccassary work that you have to do, but dont want to do. My original commitment was to own my own business. To develop my roots I had to get an education. Many would say getting an education was a goal. In some ways it was, but remember with a commitment tree were planning for a lifetime, this ws just the beginning. After I got an education I needed to get some training. I took a job with a Fortune 500 Company and received the necessary training in the printing industry. The next stage in my lifetime commitment was to gather as much knowledge in this industry as I could. I needed to have a strong root system to grow to the size I wanted. Before any tree breaks the surface and starts to grow towards the sky, it will spread a root system underground that will enable the tree to grow and become strong. The root system is actually larger than what we see above ground level. The same is true for your commitment. You must grow underground, doing the things that will align you for growth. The stronger and more dynamic the root system, the taller your commitment tree will grow.

## Questions You Should Ask Yourself

1. Write down how you want yourself to remembered.
2. What type of training and education will you need to reach the top?
3. Who can help you get to this destiny?
4. Why do you want this so bad?-What are your motives?
5. What are you willing to give up and change to obtain this?

## The Stem

Your hard work has paid off and your tree is starting to break ground. You're going in the right direction. All of your planning and preparation is paying off and you're starting the see the success of your commitment. To continue to grow your tree you to need to continue learning. The more you continue to learn, the thicker the tree trunk becomes. As the tree continues to sprout, you need to   revamp your game plan.   Develop strategies that will help you in your quest. As for me, the time was right. My game plan has been working and it was time for me to leave my job at this fortune 500 company and begin the next stage of my commitment. My tree began to blossom and I started my own business. I didn't just one day decide this is the right time, I knew because it was all part of the plan. A commitment is about planning. There isn't need for hope. Every move is strategically thought out. I developed my seed of starting my own business while in college. I didn't set a time frame on when I would own my business. I just waited for it to happen. This eliminates failure and uncertainty. Sure, many things could have derailed the growth of the tree, but there is always time to get back on track. The growing stage is so important. You must be constantly feed and nourish your tree. The more care you give it the stronger it will become.

---

### Tips

1. Listen to your heart. Is it the right thing to do at this time? As you move up the tree your strength will be tested. Determination will be the only factor that will ensure your grip and allow you to continue to climb.

2. Continue your learning. The branches of opportunity are in your sights. Don't jump for them prematurely. Don't make the wrong move, allow time for your game plan to fully develop. So many jump and all flat on their face lying there at ground level looking at having to start all over again. Patience is the key.

---

## Branches

What started out as a seed or an idea has begun to blossom to become this large tree with branches shooting out in different directions. If you stay committed, your commitment will mature and branch off, leading to more opportunities. Toys R Us went from one store that carried juvenile furniture to 811 super stores that carry toys and much more in just 49 years. Each branch in your tree represents opportunities, and as those opportunities flourish, they blossom with leaves. As I held true to my commitment to own my own business, new opportunities arose and new business ventures came about that were not related to my current business. I had to restructure my game plan, so I closed my printing business and started a new business in the medical field that had nothing to do with printing. I chose to take a new branch in my life, but that branch was still connected to the same commitment (seed) of owning my own business. In life, you are going to be faced with choices and opportunities. That is the beauty of commitments: they allow room for change. Being an optimist you know that there are always surprises around the corner. If I had set a goal to run a printing company and focused hard on just that, I would have missed out on other opportunities that proved to be more profitable and rewarding. As new challenges face you, a new branch is born and the tree becomes more developed.

## Tips

1. Welcome change with open arms. Change brings about opportunity.
2. Look for new opportunities. Take on the challenge of climbing out on a new branch.
3. Invite risk into your game plan. If you happen to fail other branches will catch your fall.

## The Forest

Isn't it amazing how long a tree can live? The stronger the commitment, the stronger your tree will become and the larger it will grow. Have you noticed that when a tree is struck by one of the most powerful bolts of electricity that only a portion of the tree will usually fall? The dead and decaying side that was directly hit will crumble. But most of the tree will remain standing.

That is true for humans and their relationships with life. Many of us will be hit by some enormous power. It will cause some to falter and some to remain standing. If you are truly committed to your game plan, you too can withstand any violent storm. There will be someone or something that will try to cut your tree down. Remember: the more dedicated you become, the greater chance of survival. You can withstand any adversity that you confront. It is time for you to plant your tree of success. A simple seed planted and well-nourished can grow to enormous heights. The minute you plant this tree you will begin to feel the power of growth. When you feel the power of growth, your enthusiasms will increase. The skies will open up and your life will begin to come together. After you have achieved all that you set to do you can look back at what started as simple idea and developed not only into a magnificent tree, but into a forest of trees. And the credit is yours.

*"The difference between ordinary and extraordinary is the little extras."*

# Chapter Five:
## Health Kicks

Have you noticed the overwhelming number of people walking around with a slight glaze in their eyes? Their fingernails are yellow, their wrinkled skin is blotchy, and when they cough, it sounds like they're going to heave their lungs out? I'm referring to smokers. Although representatives from the major cigarette manufacturers would like us to believe that cigarette smoking is not habit forming, the Surgeon General, along with thousands of other health care advisors strongly disagree. The truth is, of all the commonly known vices—smoking, drugs, and alcohol—cigarette smoking is, perhaps, one of the most addictive. I hate to admit it, but when I was a teenager I smoked cigarettes whenever I had a couple of drinks. And I don't mean Coca-Cola. I never really considered myself a smoker because my relationship with cigarettes was not an everyday thing. It's so easy to point an accusing finger at others, yet absolve yourself. I wasn't merely a "casual" cigarette smoker, I also dipped Copenhagen snuff for twelve years. My days of smoking ended during my sophomore year in college. My biology teacher, a graduate student, a man for whom I had the utmost respect, helped me to accept smoking for what it truly was. We were discussing health one day and the subject of smoking came up.

Addressing the entire class, the teacher said, "You spend a great deal of time and money to get an education and to become smarter, correct?"

We all nodded our heads in unison. Who could disagree?

"Do you consider yourself smarter than most people?" he asked.

Most of us thought he was setting us up, but the majority agreed anyway.

"Are you aware that cigarette smoking will kill you?"

After a few grunts and moans, again, a unanimous, "yes."

"So let me get this straight," the teacher continued, "All of you know that smoking will kill you, yet the majority of you continue to smoke. Is that right?"

We knew that his last question didn't need to be answered. No tricky dialogue or complicated theories. Just common sense. I knew that cigarettes killed. Everybody knew that. Reading between the lines, I discovered what my teacher was really saying: if you smoke, you are either stupid, uneducated, or both. His underlying insinuation hit a particularly sensitive nerve with me. I had always prided myself as an intelligent, logical man, always striving to be my best. Smoking was sabotaging my goal to live healthy. From that day on, I never smoked another cigarette. Sound too simple? Not really. If you take responsibility for your actions, and quit making excuses for your adverse behaviors, anything is possible.

## How to Break Any Habit Without Quitting

At first it may sound unreasonable to imagine that you can break an unpleasant habit without actually quitting, but it can be done, and less painfully than you might presume. Whether your vice is smoking, drinking, dipping snuff, chewing tobacco, or using illicit drugs, there is a method to help you successfully stop. Let's use tobacco for example. Most people who smoke or dip have at one time tried to quit. Some try quitting "cold turkey," others through hypnosis, and a majority have used such devices as the patch or nicotine gum. The problem with these methods is that the unrelenting craving predominates the temporary fix, and eventually you succumb to your longing and go back to the habit.

When you attempt to quit and fail, often your addiction worsens. Subconsciously, your body tries to make up for lost time, which may result in your habit having a tighter grip on you. There are people who have quit cold turkey. But the reason they succeeded was because they reached a crucial "breaking point." You can employ any known method, but until you reach this breaking point, it is unlikely you'll kick the habit.

When your mind and body have reached an agreement, this is the breaking point. It is a formal declaration between both, "I no longer need or want this chemical." Your mind takes a dominant role, and your body surrenders to logic. Until you reach this point, it is virtually impossible to quit an addiction. When you attempt to quit without first reaching this breaking point, your failure pushes you further away from quitting. Each battle lost reinforces your conclusion that this fight cannot be won. Why fight a hopeless battle?

Have you ever tried to quit a habit, only to be tortured by consciously obsessing about it every waking minute? Maybe instead of lighting a cigarette, you ate something. Food assumed the role as your fix. Nevertheless, your urge for nicotine was still there. The harder you tried to quit, the more powerful the addiction became. Trying to quit before you reached the breaking point completely consumed you. The sweet taste of a cigarette dominated your every thought. Everything reminded you of a cigarette. Does this scenario sound alarmingly familiar? When you reach the breaking point, your mind is at ease. The thought of a cigarette and the activities you once linked to smoking, no longer haunt you. It is like reprogramming your mind at a subconscious level. Hypnosis works much the same way. It tricks your subconscious into believing that it doesn't need a cigarette. But this method works just as effectively as hypnosis and you remain in control.

**"Through one decision alone, your life probably won't change radically, but a series of them can have an amazing effect. Every decision we make—no matter how small—leads us in one direction, either closer to our goals and wishes or further away from them."**

## Steps to Break the Habit

If you are a smoker, I have a request. Find your cigarettes and remove one from the pack. First, look at the cigarette. Don't merely glance at it, carefully examine it. Think about its origin. Use your senses; feel it; smell it. Lick the tobacco. What does it taste like? What you're holding in your hand is a sheet of paper filled with chemically treated tobacco leaves. If there is a filter, study it closely. Understand that its only purpose is to prevent some of the cancer-causing tar and other harmful toxins from polluting your body. Now, read aloud the Surgeon General's warning printed on the side of the pack. Stand in front of a mirror and grin. Has the color of your teeth changed? Look at your hands. Are your fingernails yellow? What does your breath smell like? When you cough do you feel like your lungs are trying to tell you something? Think about what they look like. Do you think your lungs are still pink and healthy, or do they look dark grey like charcoal? Now, light the cigarette. Fill your lungs to their capacity with the insidious smoke. Feel good? Taste good? As you exhale, think about how offensive the smoke smells, but don't stop.    Keep smoking.    How many packs of cigarettes do you smoke per day?  Per week?  Per year?  How much do you spend on cigarettes every year?  What could you do with the money if you had it right now?   I'm not asking you to quit smoking.   In fact, whenever you get the urge, go ahead and light up.   I want you to continue smoking. But smoke consciously.  Every time you light a cigarette, be aware of what you're doing to your teeth, skin, lungs, and all those around you—loved    ones,    family    members, friends—breathing second hand smoke.  Whenever you light a cigarette, tell yourself how vile it tastes and smells.   Every time you inhale, say it again. Go through this routine every time you have a cigarette.  After doing this for a while—each cigarette reminding you how costly and despicable a habit smoking is—without realizing it, you will gradually cut back.   You will subconsciously reprogram your mind and it will take control over your body.  Eventually, your dependency on cigarettes will disappear. Your mind will wean your body off nicotine.  You may not even notice that the number of cigarettes you smoke per day is steadily decreasing, until one day your habit is gone.

This mind-over-body technique can be used for virtually any addiction.  Don't fight it.  Just talk yourself out of it.  Let your mind convince your body that it no longer needs to support its bad habits.   And if you're one of those people who started smoking when you were a teenager, been smoking for decades, tried every method to quit, don't allow your past failures to prevent you from giving it one more try.  Remember: no matter how long you've been poisoning yourself, as soon as you quit smoking your body will begin to repair itself.

### ADD (Attention Deficit Disorder): America's most mis-diagnosed disease

In one form or another, ADD (Attention Deficit Disorder), affects more than half of all Americans. ADD is defined as: a childhood syndrome characterized by impulsiveness, hyperactivity, and short attention span, which often leads to learning disabilities and various behavioral problems. This widespread disease, if not properly treated, can result in long term consequences.  Ironically, if mis-diagnosed, the consequences can be even more devastating.  Some researchers believe ADD may be caused by  trauma at birth.  Others speculate that diet plays a major role.  Many people who have the symptoms are unaware that they might have the illness.

**"A mind is like a parachute—it functions best when open."**

**Some of the symptoms associated with ADD are:**
- Frequent day dreaming
- Inability to give close attention to detail
- Taking unexplainable risks
- Assuming  multiple tasks simultaneously, without being able to finish the majority
- Being easily distracted by external stimuli
- Hyperactivity or impulsiveness

- Inability to stop blurting out answers before questions are complete
- Evidence of clinical, social, academic, or occupational impairment
- Losing or misplacing things frequently
- Reluctance to engage in tasks that require sustained effort

**Do you possess any of the following traits?**

- Deficient in attention and effort
- Impulsive to the point of self-harm
- Problems with regulating levels of arousal
- The need for immediate reinforcement

Most would agree that to some degree, a vast majority of Americans exhibit a number of these symptoms. But not until a child is abnormally functioning in a classroom setting do educators begin to carefully monitor the child's behavior to determine if they have this disorder. Before many doctors thoroughly examine a child's behavioral patterns and characteristics, they prematurely and inconclusively diagnose ADD.

I was privileged to have had the opportunity to teach a senior class of at-risk students principles of the business world and strategies to cope with the struggles of life. These students were unable to adapt to a normal school setting. They exhibited learning disabilities, were potential dropouts, and many were disruptive in class. Some of the students diagnosed with ADD were taking medications. One girl asked me what type of student I was.

The classroom was quiet as a tomb. I saw their eyes transfixed on me, begging for an honest answer. When I announced that I had been a horrible student, their ears perked up. I told them a little story. On the last day of my junior year, I was summoned to the principal's office. Having been a less-than-exemplary student, I suspected that this meeting was not intended to honor me with commendations for excellence. I wasn't surprised to find my father waiting for me. The principal reached into his desk drawer and pulled out a hefty stack of forged notes, all written by me, and all used to excuse me from various classes. Busted. I sank into the chair, prepared to be lambasted. Strangely enough, I did not sense anger in my father. He and the principal remained remarkably composed, almost smiling. These forged excuses had made it possible for me to attend school only three days a week. In spite of my poor attendance I still managed to get passing grades in all my classes. Without saying a word, I realized that both my father and the principal were thinking the same thing: how well would I do if I really applied myself and worked hard? The principal, quite to my astonishment, asked me to sign a form. It was a formal authorization to drop out of school. I was dumbfounded.

My dad turned in the chair and glared at me. "This is not a joke. If you don't want to finish high school, this is your chance to withdraw. No strings attached. Just sign the form."

Wait a minute, I thought. All this time I'd been going to school because I thought I had to. Now they were telling me I could go home and never come back? This wasn't what I wanted. "I don't want to quit school."

"Well, you're going to have to prove that, Bryan," the principal said. "I'll give you another chance. However, unless you have a legitimate doctor's excuse, you will only be allowed to miss three days per semester. Is that clear?"

I didn't know what to say. I felt relieved, yet anxious. When my senior year had ended, I had missed only three days of school the entire year. I was nominated for the most improved student. I learned an important lesson that will follow me through life.

If you haven't already guessed, I was one of many students suffering from ADD as a child. Unfortunately, ADD hadn't yet been discovered, so my behavior was misunderstood and dealt with from an uninformed perspective. For most of my childhood years—as far back as I can remember—I had been suffering from ADD. My earliest recollection was in third grade. My teacher actually bound me to a chair to prevent me from distracting the other students.

As a result of my lifelong experience dealing with ADD, I have developed several theories about this illness that to some extent challenge those offered by orthodox medicine. First, and perhaps most consequential, when children are diagnosed with ADD they are publicly labeled as dysfunctional children. This label serves only to brand them with a feeling of inferiority.

The young woman who had asked me what kind of student I was, confessed that she had been diagnosed with ADD.  Furthermore, she'd been told that it was incurable and would be with her for the rest of her life.

I was outraged. "Who told you that?"

"My  teachers, mother, and doctors," she said.

Time for me to set the record straight.  "You're not suffering from ADD," I said.  "You're fortunate enough to be EAL.  Excited About Life."

> **"Nothing great was ever achieved**
> **without enthusiasm."**
> **Ralph Waldo Emerson**

## EAL - Excited About Life

For high functioning, enthusiastic children, why not call them Excited About Life instead of cursing them with the ADD syndrome?  When children are excited about life, their minds can juggle ten different thoughts at once.  If applied productively, this unique ability can help them to excel beyond the capabilities of "normal" children.  For people without EAL, it's difficult for them to understand its positive aspects and benefits.  As soon as I announced to that young girl that she didn't really have ADD, her face lit up and her entire demeanor changed.  For once in her life she saw herself in a different light.  She was no longer a freak; she was a gifted child.  I told her that I was proud to have EAL.  My ability to concentrate on ten different things at once created an opportunity for me to run three businesses while working to start a new one.  My mind was always racing and I wouldn't change it for the world!

In my opinion—based on first hand experience—educators today are not sufficiently trained to deal with students who are EAL. These children need to be challenged with multiple tasks and aggressive lesson plans. They can, if properly instructed, work on up to ten projects at the same time. And they can complete them quicker than a normal student working on one. These gifted students are, indeed, difficult to instruct. However, the last thing they need is to be labeled with the ADD syndrome. Furthermore, they don't need chemicals to manage their "problem." They require the proper instruction and the recognition that they are special. If you are EAL, it's time to focus your energy on positive, productive endeavors.

> *"You're not born a winner,*
> *and you were not born a loser.*
> *You are what you make yourself be."*
> **Lou Holtz**

### Tips on Managing EAL

Recite the following aloud every day:

"I possess the ability to achieve whatever I wish to accomplish, without limitation. I demand of myself persistence, excellence, and total dedication."

"I know that my attention to details is limited; therefore each day I will focus on one project for thirty minutes, free from all distractions."

"I will carry a day planner and make notations of important things to do.  I will organize and plan each activity."

## Physical Self

Do you still look the same as you did in high school?  Are you pleased with your reflection in the mirror?  Were you a lot leaner and in better shape back then?  Considering all of the fat free foods available today and America's preoccupation with living a healthful lifestyle, why aren't you in better shape?  List five reasons why you are not as fit as you want to be:

*"It's a lack of faith that makes people afraid of meeting challenges, and I believed in myself."*
*Muhammad Ali*

| List 5 Reasons Why You Are Not Fit |
|---|
| 1. |
| 2. |
| 3. |
| 4. |
| 5. |

Now, examine the five reasons listed above. Be honest with yourself. Are they legitimate reasons, or convenient excuses? Maintaining a healthy body does a lot more than attract the opposite sex. It works magic on your mind. When you feel good about yourself, your body emits a signal, and people respond favorably to this positive energy. A lion would not be king of the jungle for very long if he were sporting a pot belly and a double chin!

It would be unfair for me to make a general statement that all those out of shape do not have valid reasons. Some people have health problems or other physical ailments prohibiting them from exercising. However, if your reason is anything other than health-related, then it's just an excuse.

If you are out of shape and unhappy with the way you look, it's time to stop making excuses and get down to business.

Okay. Time to get a little tough on you. Until you accept full responsibility for the poor condition of your body, nothing will change. Accountability is what I'm talking about. Sitting in front of the T.V., munching on snacks and THINKING about exercising isn't a workable plan. No more lame excuses: it's too hot, too cold, I work too many hours, I don't have the time, maybe tomorrow, I can't leave the kids, have to maintain the house, I don't have enough energy—time to put these overused excuses to rest once and for all! No more procrastinating.

I have a simple, yet proven technique for those who are plagued with the "put-off" disease. Whenever you're faced with a task—any task—that you want to postpone, don't give yourself even a moment to manufacture excuses. JUST DO IT. At the very moment the task comes to mind, take action and get it done. I know what you're thinking: easier said than done. True. But once you see just how effective this simple technique is, you will eventually condition your mind to take responsibility and never again fall prey to the "put-off" disease.

Exercise equipment, fitness centers, and all related health care products have grown to a six-billion dollar a year industry. There is little doubt that Americans are more conscious of living healthy than ever before in history. Yet in spite of this awareness, there are a growing number of overweight and out of shape Americans. How could this be? We have become victims of our environment. On just about every street corner we find a McDonald's, Burger King, or Wendy's. As we sit in front of our big screen TV's and watch our favorite programs, we are inundated with commercials tempting us with fast foods, beer, and pop-in-the-microwave dinners. Modern supermarkets offer a full spectrum of prepared foods to make our lives a little easier. Wholesome, home cooked meals have become a faint memory for many families, particularly those where both parents have demanding careers. So, what is the answer?

Undoubtedly, the key elements to being in shape are exercise and diet. You do not need to expend endless hours working out as if you were training for the Olympics. Nor do you have to deprive yourself of the foods you enjoy. Moderation and sensibility are the operative words. With all the newfangled diets and exercise machines available today, it's easy to get confused and to conclude that staying fit is a complicated science. Nothing could be farther from the truth.

Staying fit requires only two things: commitment and common sense. Don't think of dieting as a punishment; eat what you like, but watch the calories and the saturated fat. The more you exercise, the more calories you'll burn. And your reward is being able to eat more of what you enjoy. So if you love to eat, just exercise more. Think about the joy in eating something you truly love without feeling guilty. If you crave certain foods that you know are unhealthy, apply my method to quit smoking, explained earlier in the chapter.

### *"Being Healthy is Living Healthy"*

## Time Management

By just "doing it," instead of postponing your daily tasks, you will begin to live more efficiently, which gives you more time to relax or participate in your favorite leisure activities. We live in a fast paced, high-tech society, and for most of us there never seems to be enough time in the day. Our busy lifestyles pull us in different directions and allow little time for fun. There are ways, however, to "create" more time. Over the years I have developed several simple principles that at first, may sound extreme, but if you keep an open mind most will make sense to you. By saving only fifteen minutes a day, in one year you will have saved four full days.

**1.** Schedule your next day the night before. Bring some paper and a pencil into the restroom and plan your activities for the next day. The bathroom, as strange as it may sound, is free of distractions, and will allow you to quickly organize your time.

**2.** Manage your driving time. Rather than driving to a particular destination without forethought, to avoid heavy traffic, plan your trip utilizing the most efficient route.

**3.** Silence in your car. Instead of listening to the radio, spend time focusing your thoughts on productive ideas.

**4.** Never wait on hold. When calling anyone, particularly a business that may have a number calls "stacked," don't let the operator put you on hold. Leave a brief message and move on to other tasks.

**5.** Charge others for being late. Sound ridiculous? Not really. Establish a fee structure with friends, co-workers and business associates. Time is money. For example, if you value your time at twenty-five dollars per hour, for every fifteen minutes someone is late your fee is $6.25.

**6.** Never start a meeting late. If a meeting is scheduled for eight a.m., lock the door at eight-o-one. The next time you have a meeting, everyone will know you mean business.

**7.** Always be early. Make it a habit to arrive ten minutes early. If, for some unexpected reason you will be late, always make a courtesy telephone call.

**8.** Group activities together. If you get back to your office and have a number of telephone messages, return the calls at the same time.

**9.** Don't let others keep you waiting. Order food on the way to a restaurant. Ask for the check as soon as the wait person brings your meal. How many hours have you lost in a restaurant, waiting for your check?

**10.**   Limit your casual telephone conversations. Do you have certain friends or associates who simply will not hang up?  They go on and on with hopeless drivel?  The best way to end these calls is "to interrupt yourself."   Example; "That sounds good, Jim, but I'm  sorry, I have to hang up."

**11.**   Don't waste time with small talk.  Do you have a co-worker who "camps" in your office and chats about insignificant things, while you have a stack of work to do?  Nip it in the bud: ask him what he wants and politely tell him you're too busy to chat.

**12.**    Don't waste time writing lengthy letters. Have a database of standard letters stored in your computer for all occasions.   When you need to write one, quickly personalize it and sign your name.

**13.**   Restrict T.V. time.  How many hours do you spend in front of the tube watching others live their lives while yours slips away?

**14.**   Know when to say NO!  Everybody wants a piece of your time.   Learn to say no without a detailed explanation.

**15.**   Leave your cell phone and pager off.  These high tech devices serve a useful purpose, but should be used for your convenience only.  Don't let unnecessary  interruptions steal your time.

**16.**   Make others meet your scheduling needs.  If you call a plumber, for example, and they tell you they will be there between noon and five p.m., pin them down to a specific time.  If they refuse, find someone who will conform to your schedule.

**17.**   Top off your gas at an even dollar amount. Put ten or twenty dollars in your tank so you can leave the money on the counter instead of waiting in line.

**18.**   Out source tasks beyond your capabilities. Whenever   possible—and   affordable—hire   an expert who can get a particular job finished more quickly and efficiently than you.

**19.**   Close each day prepared for the next.  Never start your day without a detailed plan.

**20.**   Don't procrastinate—**Just Do It!**

*"Action is the key to results"*

# Chapter Six:
## Love Knots;
## Building Lasting Relationships

One Saturday when I was still selling insurance, I attended an award meeting. Now normally these meetings are hopelessly boring unless you're receiving an award. But on this particular day everyone at my table, in fact, everyone in the room was entertained. We sat in awe watching an elderly couple holding hands, exchanging kisses, giggling, and discretely touching each other, acting pretty much like they had just fallen in love. For most of the six hours, completely entranced by this couple, the group at my table tried to figure out why they were so attentive toward each other. They reminded me of two teenagers on their first date. We wondered how long they'd been married. One fellow guessed they were newly weds. Another colleague was certain she was his mistress. We were all searching for answers until the couple were summoned to the podium. The speaker introduced    Mr. James and his lovely wife Margaret, and proceeded to give them an award. Mr. James had been with the company longer than any other employee.  Tonight, the speaker added, had even more significance because Mister and Mrs. James were celebrating their sixty-seventh anniversary.  I almost fell off my chair. Mr. James was eighty-six years old, and Margaret was eighty-five, yet they were as nimble and spirited as sixteen-year-olds.  When Mr. James had introduced his wife, he admiringly called her his bride.  She was, indeed, his bride!  As we watched this couple receive their award, I don't think there was a dry eye in the room.

Until that day I had no idea how to define the true meaning of love.  I'd wrestled with it my entire life.  But after observing Mr. and Mrs. James, I realized that this couple clearly represented what love was all about.  Imagine spending sixty-seven years, twenty-four-thousand, four-hundred-fifty-five days with the same person.  Seeing this extraordinary couple was an awakening for me.  At that moment I decided that I, too, wanted to feel the same passion and devotion that I was certain Mr. and Mrs. James had shared.  We should all search for a partner who touches our souls, someone to love so completely that we feel them living in our hearts with every breath.  I believe we all enter matrimony with long term hopes and limitless expectations.  But somehow we get tripped up. Enjoying a fulfilling marriage is easier than you might think.  All you need to do is have a little fun.

## Marriage - A Three-Way Street

Have you ever heard the cliche: marriage is a two-way street?  Actually, it's a three-way street. When two people meet, they're usually heading in different directions, but fate allows their lives to "collide."  When this fortuitous collision occurs, they abandon their previous routes and together head down a third path.  A fundamental of any successful marriage is to leave the past behind—the wreckage—and proceed forward, paving a new course with your life partner.  As you both head down this newly chosen path, you must remember that life does not offer the opportunity for you to make a U-turn.  As you negotiate your way through life, you will encounter many intersections.  There are right directions as well as wrong directions; the key is to read the road signs as you go.

If you were blindfolded, left in the middle of the Mojave Desert, and offered one-million dollars if you could find your way to New York in five days, do you think it would be possible?  For you to accomplish this, you'd require a compass, a detailed road map, and reliable road signs. Without these tools your trip could be treacherous.  In a relationship you must also prepare a roadway  through life that will guide you toward peace, harmony, and a mutually fulfilling marriage.  This is not a dress rehearsal; your time on Earth is limited.  Every minute is so precious that to waste even one is tragic.

Let's suppose that you were married at the age of twenty-five and lived to be sixty-five. This would mean that you were married for forty years. Follow my calculation carefully.    First let's determine how many hours you spent sleeping. For example: 8 hours a day x 7 days a week = 56 hours a week x 52 weeks a year = 2,912 hours a year x 40 years = 116,480 hours.    What this means is that you spent 13.29 years of your life asleep.    Now let's find out how many hours you spent working.    8 hours a day x 5 days a week = 40 x 52 weeks a year = 2,080 x 40 years = 83,200 hours.    9.5 years of your life were spent working. Let's roughly estimate how many hours you spent away from home.    For example: playing golf, shopping, business and social functions, traveling, etc.    Let's estimate 30 hours a week x 4 weeks = 120 hours a month x 12 =1,440 a year x 40 = 57,600 a year.    This accounts for 6.57 years of your life.    And finally, subtract some time for any miscellaneous activities that kept you away from your spouse.

**Here's the calculation:**

| | |
|---|---|
| Married: | Age 25 |
| Deceased: | Age 65 |
| Equals: | 40 years of marriage |
| Sleep: | 13.5 years |
| Equals: | 26.70 years |
| Work: | 9.5 years |
| Equals: | 17 years |
| Hours Away: | 6.5 years |
| Equals | 10.5 years |
| Misc. | 1.3 years |
| Equals | **9.2 years OF TOTAL TIME SPENT TOGETHER!** |

Isn't this calculation thought provoking? Imagine being married for forty years, yet only spending a little more than nine years with your loved one. How many of these precious years were wasted on senseless arguments, non-communication, clicking through the channels on T.V., ignoring each other? Doesn't this redefine the whole meaning of marriage? The preciousness of time? When you first fell in love and decided that you wanted to spend the rest of your life with this special person, did you realize that your time together would be so limited? If you had it to do over again would you follow the same route or drive down a more scenic path? In every relationship there will be forks in the road, winding curves, hazards, detours, and road signs. Every so often you'll get a flat tire. Once in a while your car might break down. But by working together the ride can be wonderful. "Take it slow, enjoy the ride, and read the road signs."

## Meeting Mr. or Mrs. Right

When I think about the whimsical misadventures associated with looking for Mrs. Right, I can't help but recall my teenage years. Roller skating rinks were the hottest game in town. If you wanted to meet anyone worth meeting, the elite among teenagers were hanging out at the local rink. My parents would drop me off around seven p.m. Drenched in dad's Jade East cologne, I'd be sporting my coolest duds, and my skates would be "tricked out" with the latest wheels. I can still remember the anticipation as I walked in the front door, my hormones kicking into high gear, my eyes checking out the hot chicks. As the night moved forward, the older more aggressive guys were already making their moves, marking their territory. The rest of us less suave kids watched in awe, anxiously waiting to see which girls were not spoken for. Halfway through the night the DJ's fast music surrendered to soft ballads, which was our signal that it was time for couples' skating. The moment of truth as it were. Who will ask whom to skate? As if it were yesterday I can still remember my heart hammering against my rib cage. Unlike today, a young woman never made the first move; it was an unwritten law. So the teenage girls would sit patiently, hoping that Mister Right would choose them.

What has really changed? Choosing an ideal mate is just as confusing today as it was when we were innocent kids in the roller rink. The only difference is that the stakes are much higher. But isn't it the uncertainty itself that makes love such a wondrous and exciting experience? If you are currently not in a serious relationship, then chances are you're part of the "dating scene." This can be fun, or it can be stressful. Are you meeting quality people or have your experiences been less than memorable? Have you ever noticed that the type of person you meet is in direct relationship to how you feel about yourself at that particular point in time? The way you feel inside often plays a major role in how other people see you. What you feel internally can determine who you meet. Without you realizing it, your body emits signals to other people. When you're feeling seductive, you send out signals that will attract others. But if you're not in a sociable mood, others will sense your standoffish attitude and avoid you.

## Give a Fruit Basket

When I was a bit younger I would frequent a local bar and regularly meet a group of fun loving ladies. We'd sit around, have a few laughs and enjoy a couple of cocktails. While observing the "battle of the sexes," week after week, I noticed an interesting phenomenon. Mary and Kelly—two average looking women in the group—seemed to get all the attention from eligible men. They weren't the best looking gals, yet men flocked around them as if they were movie stars. This puzzled me, so I started paying closer attention in hopes that I could solve this mystery. The more attractive women in the group believed that men did not approach them because they were actually too pretty. After careful observation I realized that looks had little to do with anything. Men approached Mary and Kelly because these women felt good about themselves and transmitted positive signals to all the men. Their happy-go-lucky, carefree spirit—along with perpetual smiles—made it easy and non-threatening for men to approach them. Guys felt compelled to talk to them. In contrast, the other girls displayed some pent up anger or ill feelings that repelled men.

What I ultimately discovered was that you must first love yourself, be happy with whom you are before you can expect others to be attracted to you. You need to spend some time alone. Examine your inner-self. Drag those skeletons out of the closets and get rid of them. Turn that frown into a smile. You might be surprised to discover that a little autonomy will yield astounding revelations about whom you really are. Find out what makes you happy. What puts a smile on your face? What are you trying to accomplish in life? You cannot attract friends or a potential lover until your life is in order and you are in touch with your feelings. Think of your thoughts as fruits in a gift basket. If the fruit is rotten, nobody will want it. If the fruit is sweet and fresh everyone will enjoy it.

## Stage the Fight - Maintain Love

Every relationship, no matter how sound, goes through rough times. Life's unexpected complications are abundant. How you manage your relationship through these unstable times will determine its success or failure. Disagreements, particularly those that escalate to intense verbal confrontations, can irrevocably damage a relationship. To avoid potentially harmful arguments, your partner and you should establish some important ground rules regarding altercations. Set a limit on how far you will allow an argument to continue. Outline parameters regarding issues about which you will and will not argue. Most important, develop a style of arguing. Discuss how you behave when you get mad, so that if you hurl a sauce pan across the room your partner won't be shocked. Define a clear set of rules that cannot be broken. By setting specific guidelines, both agreeing to the terms and conditions of this covenant, you will be able to effectively "manage" your disagreements. Establish topics that can never be brought up, or behaviors that will not be tolerated. Decide upon a mandatory resolution period. After an argument, each partner should be allowed to summarize their feelings without interruption or further debate. When it's over, sign a  peace treaty. You should also limit the amount of time you can argue. Setting parameters and defining the rules of conduct for you and your partner during confrontational times, will ensure that you build a long lasting relationship. Consider it an inexpensive insurance policy.

## The Perfect Ingredient

When love is combined with laughter, they create happiness. Laughter is an inexpensive cure for depression, stress, anger, and many illnesses. In order to laugh more, you must smile more. Abundant smiles are prerequisites to laughter. Laughter is also contagious; it has a dramatic impact on everyone around you. People are naturally drawn to those who always show those pearly-whites. And smiling is a universal language. Smile at a stranger and he smiles back. Can you imagine what you might have gotten away with when you were a child if you'd known about the power of smiling? Remember when you spilled the grape juice all over the white carpeting? You were scared to death and your face was contorted with terror. Your mother reacted to your guilty face by yelling at you and perhaps even swatting your behind. But if you would have smiled at your mom and said. "I'm sorry, Mommy. I'll help you clean it up," your mother might have reacted differently. How could she resist?

As we grow older, most of us believe that we must abandon our carefree spirits and act more seriously. I love when people urge me to behave more professionally or in a mature manner. Why would anyone want to do that? Have you ever sat in a meeting of professionals? Talk about boring. I'd rather watch grass grow! The point is this: as we grow older, the pressures and responsibilities of our everyday lives increase, which means we should smile and laugh even more than when we were children. Following are three steps to help you smile more. At first they may seem silly, but if you follow my instructions I guarantee that you'll be smiling more often.

**Step One.** Every morning before you take a shower, stand in front of a full length mirror. I'm talking about wearing only your birthday suit: absolutely buck-naked.

**Step Two.** Starting with your face, study your entire body from head to toe. What do you see? You're really no different from anyone else walking the planet, right? You might be taller, shorter, thinner, heavier—but you're just a person. Now your clothes may distinguish you from other people, but completely naked you're just like everyone else. Are you really looking at yourself?

Isn't it hysterical standing in front of that mirror completely naked? Do a little dance. Are you beginning to smile? Maybe even laughing?

**Step Three.** Are you ready to really giggle? Good. Stand as close as you can to the mirror without your eyes crossing. Now smile as big as you can, stretch those lips until it hurts and hold it for thirty seconds. Repeat this three times. When you're driving to work, remember that silly grin. When you're sitting in that never-ending sales meeting, recall that exaggerated smile. No matter what you do throughout the day, keep the image of you standing in front of the mirror in the forefront of your mind. Smile at everyone you see. Observe how many people smile back. After conducting your smile survey for one week, spend one day not smiling and pay close attention to everyone's unusual reaction.

### *"The only difference between a good day and a bad day, is your ATTITUDE!"*

### Take on New Challenges

In an effort to keep your relationship fresh and exciting, your partner and you should always search for new adventurous activities that will help your relationship reach new levels of excitement. Have you ever sat in a restaurant and observed a couple sitting across from each other with barely a word shared between them? Relationships become commonplace because couples do not expend enough energy looking for mutually enjoyable activities. Often they fall into ruts, participating in the same activities over and over, without diversity. When the thrill is gone, relationships become boring. Try new restaurants, take a class together, do something you've never done before. Consider taking on a new hobby that would be fun for both of you. Whether it's playing golf, tennis, sailing around the world, or backpacking in the mountains, search for activities that stimulate your senses and inject a little passion into your partnership.

> *"If at first you don't succeed,*
> *try to hide your astonishment."*
> **Harry F. Banks**

## Grow Together

Each day you are faced with new experiences that will either enrich or hinder your life. Positive experiences help you to grow, while negative ones restrict you. Although no two people are alike, in order for a relationship to flourish, both partners need to mature at a similar pace. Without this harmonious evolution, you might awaken one morning, and realize that neither of you knows who the other really is. One way to ensure continued compatibility and strengthen your bond is to share each other's experiences by frequently talking openly about them, without restrictions or limitations. Nothing cultivates a more vibrant relationship than forthright communication. Getting to know each other is a work in progress; it never ends. And remember: no matter how well you think you know your mate, with each new day you will discover a nuance in your partner that didn't exist yesterday.

## Money

Second only to infidelity, money problems cause more divorces in America than any other factor. Financial hardship in a marriage produces an enormous amount of stress. Stress fosters negative emotions and these emotions can tear two people apart. No matter how sound the marriage, or deep the love, the pressure is almost insurmountable. As one of the major reasons for divorce, you should establish money ground rules early in a marriage. Decisions on purchasing high ticket items should be jointly considered. Investment strategies, retirement objectives, and all financial priorities should be clearly outlined and agreed upon. If you encounter financial difficulties, work as a team to remedy your problems. Take measures to ensure that this condition is temporary. Above all, avoid making the same mistakes twice. A well-thought out plan is the key.

*"Money never starts an idea:*
*it is the idea that starts the money."*
**W. J. Cameron**

## Free Yourself from Emotional Disaster

You cannot maintain a productive relationship if negative emotions interfere with your happiness. Sustained anger, jealousy, hatred, or envy only serves to jeopardize your marriage. Negative emotions will destroy even the heartiest relationship. Furthermore, there is a definitive distinction between love and possession. Wanting to possess your partner is unhealthy. These negative emotions do not appear randomly; they exist because an event from the past is living in the present. To free yourself from negative emotions you must spend some time self-evaluating your behavior. You must explore the reasons why you feel something is lacking in your life, or what might have happened that caused you to act this way. Negative emotions are often triggered by your subconscious mind. The best way for you to manage and control negative emotions is to refer to chapter three and reread the section entitled, Methods to Overcome Negative Thoughts.

> *"The pessimist sees difficulty in every opportunity, the optimist sees opportunity in every difficulty."*
> **L. P. Jacks**

## Three Powerful Words: I Love You

The words, I love you are, perhaps, the most beautiful words in the English language. They have the power to heal, and can never be called upon too often.  The first and last words out of your mouth every day should be I love you. Shower your partner with endless salutations of I love you.  Say it the moment you walk in the door and the moment before you leave.  Be creative and playful; hide love notes in their coat pocket or under their pillow.  Place a provocative note in a briefcase to give your partner something to think about.  Show your love with hugs and kisses.  A kiss on the cheek can turn a bad day into a happy one.     Be   spontaneous   and   unpredictable. Surprise your partner by doing the unexpected. By declaring and showing your love, your relationship will be filled with passion and joy.

*"The most wonderful and beautiful things in the world cannot be seen nor touched, but are felt with the heart."*

## Recovering From a Breakup or Divorce

Surviving a failed relationship is a formidable challenge.  After sharing your life with another human being, giving your love and devotion to that   special   person,   breaking   up   can   be devastating.  You put so much time and effort into building a long term relationship, which when it's over, you feel profound emptiness.  Open wounds do not heal easily.   You may find yourself vulnerable and insecure, and in some cases emotionally dysfunctional.   When there is a breakup there are no winners or losers; both of you lose.  But in time you can be a winner.  This may, at first, sound unreasonable, but if you face a breakup in a productive way, it may prove to be the best thing that ever happened to you.

**Allow Yourself Time to Heal.** After a relationship ends, many people are inclined to immediately get involved with another partner.   It's difficult to awaken every morning alone when you were accustomed to cuddling with your mate.  To begin a transitional relationship only serves to postpone the healing process.  You cannot give yourself to another, without reservation or limitation, unless you have dealt with the issues that caused your relationship to end.  Postponing the inevitable by getting involved with another before you have sufficiently healed will most certainly sabotage any possibility that this relationship can work.  You cannot bring old baggage to a new relationship. You must take some time for self-evaluation. Until you learn more about yourself, and are happy with whom you are, you will be unable to begin a new relationship.  With each day that passes, you will move one step closer to healing.

**A Prescription for Heartache:** Exercise. Nothing helps heal the psyche more effectively than physical exertion.  By developing an aggressive workout program that requires great effort and commitment, you will heal your emotional wounds more quickly.  Whether you lift weights, attend an aerobics class, jog, rollerblade, or climb mountains, exercise will make you feel good about yourself.   I would also suggest that you join various groups that are involved in activities you enjoy.  Now is that time.

**Allow Yourself to Morn.** When you feel the urge to cry, don't suppress it.   Give yourself the opportunity to feel sorrow.  Crying is a necessary part of the healing process.

**Tell Yourself it's Okay.**   Do not, under any circumstances overanalyze your failed relationship and drive yourself mad trying to figure out what you did wrong.   For whatever reason, you and your partner were incompatible and no one is to blame.  Do reflect back and take an inventory of those things you liked.  Remember these positive things and bring them to your next relationship.

**Blow out the Torch.**  Do not torture yourself with unrealistic expectations that your relationship can be reconciled.  Blow the thought out of your head and move on.  Even if you get back together, you might find yourself immersed in the same quicksand.   It is almost always best to move forward.   If it's possible for you to preserve a friendship with your ex-lover, without causing you undue   heartache,   by   all   means   continue interacting with this person.   But under no circumstances should you live in the past. Remember: time will heal all. You have my word on that.

> *"You can not change your past,*
> *but you use your past to help you*
> *move into tomorrow."*

# Chapter Seven:
## The Vacation

Imagine winning a free trip to the most beautiful island in the world. The island is surrounded by lush mountain ranges and vast beaches with crystal white sand. The weather never varies: eighty degrees, sun-rich skies, cool ocean breezes. Envision lying on the beach with your feet buried in the cool sand, the ocean air fills your lungs, you sip a refreshing pina colada. The sun, low in the western sky, begins its descent toward the water. As you observe another breathtaking sunset, you remember that you have absolutely nothing to do. No deadlines. No homework. No pressing obligations. You don't have to answer to anyone. You can go hiking, swimming, snorkeling, fishing or choose to lazily lie on the sand. Can you smell the ocean air? Feel a gentle breeze tousle your hair? Your mind is totally at ease, as serene as a pond on a summer night. Your life is stress-free and tranquil. As you muse through your memory bank, think about how you felt during your last vacation. What was going through your mind the very first day? Can you remember five things that made you smile? Write them down.

| List 5 Things That Made You Smile |
| --- |
| 1. |
| 2. |
| 3. |
| 4. |
| 5. |

I'd be willing to bet that most of you enjoyed a wonderful experience on your last vacation. You probably didn't wear a watch, stayed out till the wee hours of morning, slept in until noon, and most certainly, you smiled more than usual. Why does that vacation have to be so much different from everyday life?

When you're on vacation, you feel reborn, supercharged with energy and enthusiasm. Even if some angry, inconsiderate person cut you off on the highway, you'd probably wave and smile. Things that might ordinarily upset you seem inconsequential. Nothing could ruin your day. While standing in line at the local grocery store, instead of losing your patience and glaring at your watch every two minutes, worrying about having to be somewhere, you smile at people and whistle a happy tune. When your vacation ends and you're sitting on the plane flying back home, you promise yourself, like you have so many times before, that somehow, some way you're going to take a vacation every month because relaxation and a carefree existence are truly what life is all about. But two weeks later when someone else cuts you off on the highway, your vacation is quickly forgotten and you make an obscene gesture and scream profanities that only you can hear. All those promises are now a faint memory. Back in the same rut. Another year of stress and tension and pressure passes and you find yourself whispering a familiar line: "I need to save some money, so I can take a vacation."

Believe it or not, the beautiful island you envisioned can be part of your life every single day. You don't have to go anywhere to be on vacation. Outside influences will try to spoil your vacation, but it's your responsibility to maintain your happy spirit. You are in control. Only you can determine whether you live your life on a never-ending vacation or surrender to all those external forces trying to make your time here on Earth trying.

Not too long ago I was flying from Dallas to Atlanta early in the morning. I was surprised that this seven-twenty flight was full. Sitting in front of me were two big men, one looked to be in his late fifties, the other I'd guessed was in his earlier thirties. They didn't stop talking for the entire flight.  I felt uncomfortable eavesdropping, but what choice did I have in such confined quarters? They discussed many topics, but for two grueling hours I heard them bellyache about El Nino, particularly how it adversely affected so many cities in different regions of the country.  Can you imagine listening to two people whine about such a depressing topic for two solid hours?  Why would anyone want to engage in such a negative conversation for two hours?

I've always been rather curious with people who enjoy talking about negative events over which they have no control.  What do they hope to accomplish?  Talking about such things jeopardizes your vacation.  Conversations should be focused on productive things that can be changed, fixed, modified, improved or positively influenced, matters in which you can participate. What is the benefit of wasting precious time and getting worked up over circumstances you cannot control?  If you had only one year to live would you waste even a minute on hopeless drivel? Actions speak louder than words.  Be a "mover and shaker," make things happen through actions.  Face life with enthusiasm.  Enthusiasm moves mountains.

## Enthusiasm

When you awaken every morning do you jump out of bed, ready to tackle a new, exciting day?  Or do you lie there for a while wishing you could roll over and go back to sleep?  If you don't face each day with anticipation and enthusiasm, you're probably in a rut. Your raft may have hit bottom. Time for you to move your raft toward deeper waters. You cannot reach your Lake of Dreams without getting your raft back into the current. Following are eighteen warning signs that your raft has hit bottom.

Going to work doesn't excite you.
Not enough time in each day.
You walk around staring at the floor.
Your energy level has noticeably decreased.
Your life lacks thrills or adventure.
Your sex drive has lessened; it's become routine.
You feel as though your life has no direction.
You've become more introverted.
Use of alcohol, drugs, or tobacco has increased.
You never stop to "smell the flowers."
You feel overwhelmed with anxiety.
You fear you're losing control.
Your eating habits have dramatically changed.
Friends and family members avoid you.
You're experiencing financial pressure.
Frequent confrontations with immediate family.
You feel as though you're constantly under pressure.
You can't remember the last time you laughed.

## How to Develop an Unlimited Reserve of Enthusiasm and Energy

The Formula:
Enthusiasm x Optimism + Hope = Success

A lack of enthusiasm is usually associated with a dismal outlook on life. Your perception is that you have nothing to look forward to, therefore you're apathetic. If you are lacking enthusiasm, it is likely that factors deemed beyond your control are repressing you. As simplistic as it may sound, perception is reality; change your perception and you change your reality. Enthusiasm creates energy; energy is the engine that propels your life forward. Positive things will happen in your life when you possess a high level of energy. Success and energy are synonymous. Enthusiastic people are usually successful. When an enthusiastic person walks into a gloomy room, their energy is like a bright light. It affects everybody in a positive way. Enthusiasm is also highly contagious.

## How to Become Enthusiastic

Enthusiasm is a characteristic you can learn to develop. It is a byproduct of happiness. Following are some suggestions to help you ignite and maintain a high level of enthusiasm.

**Give Thanks** — Every night before you fall asleep give thanks for having lived one more day. Be grateful that you had another opportunity to participate in the wonder of life. Look forward to tomorrow, anticipating another opportunity to sip the nectar of life.

**Self Talk** — Each morning when you awaken, before facing your day, have a little pep-talk with yourself. Acknowledge all the wonderful things in your life. Reflect for a moment on those things you cherish most. Be thankful that today is another day of vacation. Do not think about the problems or obligations facing you today. By maintaining a high level of enthusiasm these tasks can be easily managed. Start the day on a positive note. An enthusiastic attitude begins long before your feet hit the floor.

**Your Diet** — I cannot stress enough how vitally important your diet is. You are, indeed what you eat. One of the most effective ways to increase your enthusiasm is to increase your energy. To accomplish this you must maintain the proper diet. Have you ever eaten a hearty lunch, returned to the office, and spent the rest of the day trying to keep your eyes open? Ideally, you should eat a well-balanced, substantial breakfast and a moderate lunch and dinner. In between, enjoy a couple of healthy snacks. If you eat reasonable portions five or six times a day your energy level will increase because your metabolism will work at a steady rate. Meals low in carbohydrates are preferred.

**The "I Am" Principle** — Frequent declarations will help you to maintain enthusiasm and energy. "I am the most enthusiastic, motivated, energetic person in the world." Say this out loud—and mean it! Whenever you want to alter your behavior and attitudes convince yourself you're already that way. If you feel yourself slowing, tell yourself, "I am an unstoppable energy machine ready for action." No matter what characteristic you wish to develop, picture yourself the way you want to be and declare it. Repeat the affirmation until you believe it. Eventually, you will enhance your self-esteem and positively influence everyone you encounter.

**New Challenges** — Most people are creatures of habit and comfort levels; they are resistant to change. But taking on new challenges taxes your creativity, sharpens your instincts, and provides a platform to increase your knowledge. New experiences tap into the super powers that are tucked away in your subconscious brain. Whether you pursue a new hobby or activity, start a new business, or volunteer your time for a worthy cause, challenging yourself every day makes your life more meaningful.

**Meet New People** — Whether at school, work, or social gatherings, every day you interact with people—some familiar, others for the first time. Most of the people you encounter are merely acquaintances, but you can choose, if you wish, to create more meaningful relationships by getting to know selected people on a more personal level. This does not suggest that you should pursue intimate friendships randomly. However, if there are interesting people around you and you haven't yet explored the possibility of a more nourishing friendship, by all means make a positive gesture toward that end. Seeking new friendships will help develop your "positive optimistic personality." In other words, when you're getting to know someone you are usually on your best behavior. As you go through the process of getting to know each other, conversations will be naturally more focused on positive issues, which almost completely precludes the possibility for negative or non-productive dialogue.

**Sing the Song of Enthusiasm** — If at any point during the day you feel logy or unusually unmotivated, stop whatever you're doing, bend your knees and crouch down like a baseball player waiting for a ground ball. Clap your hands and say, "If I act enthusiastic I'll be enthusiastic. I'm number ONE!" Repeat this rhythmic chant until you remove all negative thought and recharge your energy level. Are folks going to look at you a little strangely? Sure. But who cares?

> **"The man who believes he can do something is probably right, and so is the man who believes he can't."**

### Establish Strong Values

To maintain and propel your motivation and enthusiasm you must establish strong values. Values are principles, standards, or qualities considered worthwhile or desirable. Well-defined values will help you build a strong foundation upon which you can build a more meaningful life. Values—more clearly defined—are your self-worth. Your beliefs and the manner in which you choose to represent yourself will determine how others see you.

The next time you're chatting with a friend ask him or her what they stand for, what factors make them who they are? You might be shocked to learn that few people can answer this question without great difficulty. When was the last time you asked yourself this question? What are your values and how do they impact your behavioral patterns? Are you the best person you can be? Think about what makes you a great person. List five values that are most important to you. For example: Honesty, Respect, Dedication, Loyalty, Devotion.

| List 5 Values Most Important to You |
| --- |
| 1. |
| 2. |
| 3. |
| 4. |
| 5. |

Now that you've established your five most important values, elaborate by putting them into sentence form. For example: I always conduct myself in an honest way. I treat others with respect. I am dedicated to increase my knowledge and understanding of the world. I am a loyal husband, father and friend. I am devoted to doing the best I can at everything I do. Now recite your values aloud. Repeat them several times, each time a little louder. Don't you feel energized? From this day forward make a commitment to consider your values before taking action or making consequential decisions. Establishing values is vitally important. They go hand in hand with establishing a Commitment Tree. Although a commitment tree gives you direction, values will determine how far up the tree you go. If your value system establishes strong self-worth and a high level of confidence, your enthusiasm will never betray you.

## Establishing Values Can be Dangerous

There is one common pitfall to establishing values and living by them: some people have a tendency to impose their beliefs on others. Usually the people closest to you get the brunt of this well-intended assault: friends, family, neighbors, class mates—anyone who might listen to your self-proclaimed omnipotence. It is normal to feel passionate about your values, but don't feel so strongly that you fail to recognize that others have their own perspectives and viewpoints and value systems, and it is neither your job nor your place to convert them to your system. Some people may have no system, and in a broad sense not having a value system IS their value system. It is likely that your life partner may share many of your values, but still, each of us is as individual as a fingerprint and no two people categorically share the same value system.  It is often difficult for us to accept that our values don't work for everyone; what's important in our life may be insignificant to others.

I have a great friend who enjoys the night life. Although we share a number of values, we do not agree on how to spend our evenings and mornings.  He lives for the weekends, and loves dining and drinking all hours of the night.  If there's a party anywhere you can be sure he'll be there.  I, on the other hand prefer quieter evenings.  I especially enjoy a good night's sleep, rising early, having a hearty breakfast, and watching the sun rise while sipping a cup of robust coffee.

One evening not too long ago, my friend and I had a telephone conversation and decided to play a round of golf the following morning.  We both loved playing early, when the ground was still moist and the sun was just peeking over the horizon, so I scheduled an eight a.m. tee off time. Having had an active week, I ate an early dinner, read a book until my eyes were drooping, and retired early.  The next morning I arrived at the club at six a.m., ate a big breakfast, and hit a bucket of golf balls to tune up my swing. When I'd finished, it was seven a.m. and my friend still hadn't arrived.  I called his home and was surprised and annoyed to hear him answer the telephone.

"Are we still playing golf?" I asked.  My voice was impatient.

I heard him yawn into the phone. "Yeah. Um . . . I'll be there in a few minutes."

I hung up the telephone, shook my head and mumbled to myself. After pacing the club house floor for fifteen minutes, feeling like an expectant father, my friend came strolling in the door as if he were two hours early! He looked like he'd been run over by a fleet of Army trucks.

"Glad you could finally make it," I said. My voice was tight.

He shook his head. "You won't believe what happened last night. You should have been there. It was absolutely crazy."

"Don't you think it's time you grew up and changed your lifestyle?" I said. "You can't spend the rest of your life partying and hanging out in bars." I looked into his eyes and realized I'd stepped over the line.

In my own self-righteous way I was blinded by a desire to "fix" my friend's life. I tried to impose my belief system on him. Granted, I cared about him and was deeply concerned for his welfare, but I didn't have the right to meddle in his life. Do you see how easily good intentions can turn bad? There is a monumental lesson to be learned here, one that will impact your relationships in a most profound way. Accept your family and friends for whom they are. Help if you are asked, but let them live their lives as emancipated human beings. Love them, cherish them, comfort them, offer your unrestricted support, but never forget that your role is not to police their lives.

### *"Live life as if tomorrow was your last day."*

## Some Final Thoughts

You now have much to think about, consequential decisions to make.  If you are satisfied with your life, I applaud you and wish you well.  I suspect, though, that you, like most people are seeking to improve your existence.  Even the most exemplary life can use a little polish.  No one walking this planet has all the answers, but I truly hope that sharing my life experiences with you and outlining those philosophies that have helped me with my journey to the Lake of Dreams can impact you in a significant way.

One of the most important lessons to be learned is to understand that life has little to do with the final destination.  We will all get there soon enough.  Life is truly the trip and you must cherish each moment.  Live life as it comes: one day at a time.  Be the best you can be and your presence on this planet will remain immortal.  Your wisdom and knowledge will be handed down and live on for future generations.

As I write these final thoughts, I am reminded of a Dear Abby column published many years ago.  An unfortunate man, barely middle age and tragically lying on his death bed, wrote a letter to Abby expressing his thoughts on life.  During his final hours he realized, much to his dismay, that those things most important to him had played a very small role in his life as a husband and father.  He painfully understood that all the activities he cherished most had been free, yet he had squandered countless opportunities to spend quality time with his family and participate in their lives. You see, this poor soul was so busy running in the rat race of life that he hadn't allocated sufficient time to enjoy the true pleasures of life. It was a brutal commentary on a wasted life. Abby's reply was poignant indeed. She told the man that in over twenty years of writing her column, she had received dozens of similar letters from people on their death beds. All of them had shared the same startling revelation: they had learned much too late that the best things in life are free, and that all the money in the world could not give them a second chance to live their lives more wisely. She added, ironically, that no one had ever expressed regret that they hadn't worked more overtime, or bought more material things.

## Wisdom from an Indian Elder

It doesn't interest me what you do for a living.  I want to know what you ache for, and if you dare to dream of meeting your heart's longing.

It doesn't interest me how old you are.  I want to know if you will risk looking like a fool for love, for your dreams, for the adventure of Being alive.

It doesn't interest me what planets are squaring your moon.  I want to know if you have touched the center of your own sorrow, if you have been opened by life's betrayals or have become shriveled and closed from fear of further pain!

I want to know if you can sit with pain, mine and your own, without moving to hide it or fix it.

I want to know if you can be with joy, mine and your own; if you can dance with wildness and let the ecstasy fill you to the tips of your fingers and toes without cautioning us to be careful, be realistic, or to remember the limitations of being human.

It doesn't interest me if the story you're telling me is true.  I want to know if you can disappoint another to be true to yourself; if you can bear the accusation of betrayal and not betray your own soul.

I want to know if you can be faithful and therefor be trustworthy.

I want to know if you can see beauty even when it is not pretty every day, and if you source your life from God's presence.

I want to know if you can live with failure, yours and mine, and still stand on the edge of a lake and shout to the silver of the moon, Yes! I'm alive.

It doesn't interest me to know where you live or how much money you have.

I want to know if you can get up after the night of grief and despair, weary and bruised to the bone, and do what needs to be done for the children.

It doesn't interest me who you are, how you came here. I want to know if you stand in the center of the fire with me and not shrink back.

It doesn't interest me where or what or with whom you have studied. I want to know what sustains you from the inside when all else falls away.

I want to know if you can be alone with yourself, and if you truly like the company you keep in the empty moments.

**Oriah Mountain Dreamer, Indian Elder.**

# Just a
Thought

# Just a Thought

# Just a Thought

# Just a Thought

# Just a
# Thought

# Just a
# Thought

# Just a
# Thought

# Just a
# Thought

# Just a
## Thought

# Just a
# Thought

# Quick Order Form

**Fax orders:** (972) 233-2738. Send this form.

**Telephone orders**: Call 214-394-8262

**E-Mail:** bbforms@ix.netcom

**Postal orders:** Simple Publishing, Bryan Fiese
P.O Box 701774, Dallas, Tx 75370

**Please send the following Books or Tapes.**

_____

_____

_____

**Please send more FREE information on**:
❑ Other books,   ❑ Tapes,   ❑ Seminars/Speaking
❑ Coaching sessions

**Name:**_____

**Address:**_____

**City:**_____ **State:**_____ **Zip**_____

**Telephone:**_____

**e-mail address**:_____

**Sales Tax**: Please add 8.25% for products shipped to Texas addresses.

**Shipping:** $4 for first book or tape and $2.00 for each additional product.

**International**: $9 for 1st book or tape: $5 for each additional.

**Payment:**       ❑ Check,        ❑ Credit Card
❑ Visa,       ❑ MasterCard,   ❑ AMEX

**Card Number:**_____

**Name on card:**_____

**Expiration date:**_____ /_____

# Quick Order Form

**Fax orders:** (972) 233-2738. Send this form.

**Telephone orders**:  Call 214-394-8262

**E-Mail:** bbforms@ix.netcom

**Postal orders:** Simple Publishing, Bryan Fiese
P.O Box 701774, Dallas, Tx 75370

**Please send the following Books or Tapes.**

_____

_____

_____

**Please send more FREE information on**:
❑ Other books,   ❑  Tapes,      ❑ Seminars/Speaking
❑ Coaching sessions

**Name:**_____

**Address:**_____

**City:**_____ **State:**_____ **Zip**_____

**Telephone:**_____

**e-mail address**:_____

**Sales Tax**: Please add 8.25% for products shipped to Texas addresses.

**Shipping:** $4 for first book or tape and $2.00 for each additional product.

**International**: $9 for 1st book or tape: $5 for each additional.

**Payment:**      ❑ Check,      ❑ Credit Card
❑ Visa,      ❑ MasterCard,    ❑ AMEX

**Card Number:**_____

**Name on card:**_____

**Expiration date:**_____ /_____

# Quick Order Form

**Fax orders:** (972) 233-2738. Send this form.

**Telephone orders:** Call 214-394-8262

**E-Mail:** bbforms@ix.netcom

**Postal orders:** Simple Publishing, Bryan Fiese
P.O Box 701774, Dallas, Tx 75370

**Please send the following Books or Tapes.**

_____

_____

_____

**Please send more FREE information on:**
❑ Other books,   ❑ Tapes,       ❑ Seminars/Speaking
❑ Coaching sessions

**Name:**_____

**Address:**_____

**City:**_____ **State:**_____ **Zip**_____

**Telephone:**_____

**e-mail address**:_____

**Sales Tax**: Please add 8.25% for products shipped to Texas addresses.

**Shipping:** $4 for first book or tape and $2.00 for each additional product.

**International**: $9 for 1st book or tape: $5 for each additional.

**Payment:**      ❑ Check,        ❑ Credit Card
❑ Visa,      ❑ MasterCard,   ❑ AMEX

**Card Number:**_____

**Name on card:**_____

**Expiration date:**_____ /_____

# Quick Order Form

**Fax orders:** (972) 233-2738. Send this form.

**Telephone orders:** Call 214-394-8262

**E-Mail:** bbforms@ix.netcom

**Postal orders:** Simple Publishing, Bryan Fiese
P.O Box 701774, Dallas, Tx 75370

**Please send the following Books or Tapes.**

_____
_____
_____
_____

**Please send more FREE information on:**
❑ Other books,    ❑ Tapes,      ❑ Seminars/Speaking
❑ Coaching sessions

**Name:**_____

**Address:**_____

**City:**_____ **State:**_____ **Zip**_____

**Telephone:**_____

**e-mail address:**_____

**Sales Tax:** Please add 8.25% for products shipped to Texas addresses.

**Shipping:** $4 for first book or tape and $2.00 for each additional product.

**International:** $9 for 1st book or tape: $5 for each additional.

**Payment:**     ❑ Check,     ❑ Credit Card
❑ Visa,      ❑ MasterCard,    ❑ AMEX

**Card Number:**_____

**Name on card:**_____

**Expiration date:**_____/_____